A Spirituality for BROKENNESS

DISCOVERING YOUR DEEPEST SELF IN DIFFICULT TIMES

Terry Taylor

Walking Together, Finding the Way®
SKYLIGHT PATHS®
PUBLISHING
Woodstock, Vermont

A Spirituality for Brokenness:
Discovering Your Deepest Self in Difficult Times

2009 Quality Paperback Edition, First Printing
©2009 by Terry Taylor

Library of Congress Cataloging-in-Publication Data
Taylor, Terry, 1951–
  A spirituality for brokenness : discovering your deepest self in difficult times / Terry Taylor.—Quality pbk. ed.
       p. cm.
  Includes bibliographical references.
  ISBN-13: 978-1-59473-229-4 (quality pbk.)
  ISBN-10: 1-59473-229-9 (quality pbk.)
  1. Spirituality. 2. Spiritual life. I. Title.
  BL624.T398 2009
  204'.42—dc20

                                                                    2009003775

10 9 8 7 6 5 4 3 2 1

Manufactured in the United States of America
Cover design: Jenny Buono

SkyLight Paths is creating a place where people of different spiritual traditions come together for challenge and inspiration, a place where we can help each other under-stand the mystery that lies at the heart of our existence.

SkyLight Paths sees both believers and seekers as a community that increasingly tran-scends traditional boundaries of religion and denomination—people wanting to learn from each other, *walking together, finding the way*.

SkyLight Paths, "Walking Together, Finding the Way" and colophon are trademarks of LongHill Partners, Inc., registered in the U.S. Patent and Trademark Office.

Walking Together, Finding the Way®
Published by SkyLight Paths Publishing
A Division of LongHill Partners, Inc.
Sunset Farm Offices, Route 4, P.O. Box 237
Woodstock, VT 05091
Tel: (802) 457-4000   Fax: (802) 457-4004
www.skylightpaths.com

To Mary Ellen Cozad Taylor,
who gave birth to me and whose spirit
served as midwife to this book.

The very time I thought I was lost,
The dungeon shook, and my chains fell off....
—from a nineteenth-century spiritual

Contents

Acknowledgments

I cannot adequately express my gratitude to my partner, Fran Englander, for all that she contributed to this book. I would also like to express deep thanks to my friend and spiritual advisor, Joe Grant. Among those I wish to acknowledge for their key role in bringing this book to print are my editor, Marcia Broucek, and her predecessor, Mark Ogilbee.

A number of friends and mentors have nurtured me over the years with their kindness and love: Miss Merita Levine; Sr. Josepha McNutt, MSBT; my Aunt Helen Murdock; Leonard Cox; Mimi Ferry; David Cook; Jim Douglass; Fr. John Dear, SJ; Cindy Humbert; mentors Robert and Ruth Brooker; friend and collaborator Hollinger Bernard; my fifth-grade teacher (known to me only as Miss Putney); and my seventh-grade English teacher, Beverly Silvasi. I also wish to thank Thomas Merton, Ram Dass, and Claire van Vliet for their creative inspiration. I am indebted to Dr. Steve McCabe (my hand specialist) and Rhonda Curry (my hand therapist) for helping me to mend physically. And finally I want to thank Anita Mclaughlin, Don Feeney, and all the other pilgrims who have been part of my mending journey. Even though this book is dedicated to my mother, its healing spirit flows from my father, Carl Taylor, who became my friend when I was in my thirties.

Introduction

Many of us who feel broken on the inside seem to be perfectly okay on the outside. We don't necessarily suffer from injury or illness; our lives may not have been turned upside down by catastrophe. Yet we still feel a sense of alienation or separateness from the world around us. Perhaps you are among the thousands who just *feel* broken and can't explain why. You may not have a dramatic story or traumatic past, yet you may feel out of sync with friends, family—even yourself.

As I crossed the threshold of my fiftieth birthday, I began to have a more urgent sense of brokenness, a feeling that has plagued me my entire life. And as I talked with friends, I found, to my surprise, that many, if not most, of them also felt broken in some way—not acceptable to others or themselves. I learned that many people suffered the way I did:

- The woman who has struggled with eating disorders all of her adult life;
- The couple who, after working for thirty years in the same jobs at the same company, were both fired when the plant closed;
- The talented athlete who, because of an automobile accident injury, can no longer compete and feels that her life has lost its meaning;

1

- The eighty-two-year-old man who fought his way across Europe in World War II and has since spent his life trying to come to grips with what he did in the war and what the war did to him;
- The brilliant young man born with cerebral palsy who cannot find a productive livelihood;
- The woman who seems to find herself in abusive relationships over and over again;
- The young man who has always felt unaccepted within his family because his mother was a prostitute;
- The young woman who witnessed her older brother's suicide when she was only twelve and has felt responsible for his death all her life;
- The many men, women, and children I know who have experienced violence (physical, mental, emotional, or sexual) directed at them or their loved ones.

Most of us who feel broken try to find something or someone that will fix, repair, or heal that sense of brokenness. Unfortunately, that search is more often than not fruitless. What *is* fruitful is the journey inward to name and understand our brokenness so we can begin the mending process. What we need are clear-eyed and kindhearted ways of understanding and moving through our brokenness.

The great psychologist Carl Jung once said that in all of his years as a therapist, he had never encountered anyone whose problem, at its core, was not fundamentally spiritual. If our problems are fundamentally spiritual, then it would seem reasonable, even necessary, to use powerful spiritual tools to address them.

In my search for ways to alleviate my own anguish, and perhaps that of others, I have explored many spiritual tools from the world's great religions. As the director of Interfaith Paths to Peace, my work is to bring practitioners of different religions together for events that will spark dialogue and better understanding. Over the years, I have heard how brokenness is felt by men, women, and children around the globe. I have experienced the power and richness of Hinduism, Judaism, Buddhism, Islam, and other religions. I have learned that we can encounter the transcendent in the midst of our lives, whether we live on the magical Celtic island of Iona or on the banks of the Ohio River, where I currently reside. And I have come to discover many healthy spiritual practices that help people deal with problems in their daily lives.

The walls that have traditionally separated the world's religions are becoming porous, allowing spiritual tools and practices to flow between and among them. I find Protestant friends embracing the Christian Orthodox practice of repeating the Jesus Prayer. I know Jews who embrace Buddhist meditation practices. I know Catholics who employ the Prayer to the Four Directions from Native American spirituality. More than at any other time in history, we now have the possibility of using spiritual tools and practices from *all* religions to address our brokenness in ways that we might never have thought possible a generation ago.

As I have looked further into these many religious traditions, I have begun to understand that if we turn to a spirituality uniquely tuned for times of brokenness, we can transform our moments of supreme vulnerability into opportunities for unhindered reflection and spiritual growth. As I began to find spiritual tools that helped me, I started offering a workshop titled "A Spirituality for Brokenness." Just as I clarify at each workshop, I'll be up front with you: I am not offering "healing." I am not an "authority." But I have lived, and am living, this journey of mending, and I will give you as honest a version as I can of what has helped me and, I believe, can help you with your own journey.

I have found seven steps in particular that have helped me formulate a spirituality for brokenness, and I want to share them with you in this book:

1. *Recognize your brokenness:* The often-neglected tradition from the Jewish and Christian faiths of taking a Sabbath or a regular period of rest and reflection is a simple practice (but often difficult to actually *do*) that can help you suspend judgment about your situation and see your

brokenness more clearly, which will have a profound effect on your attitude toward it.

2. *Have compassion for your brokenness:* The Tibetan Buddhist practices of *maitri* and *tonglen* are two inter-related meditation techniques that can help you gain a deeper and more compassionate awareness of your bro-kenness, and the brokenness of others.

3. *Understand your brokenness:* The Christian method of *Lectio Divina*, which is essentially an expanded way of studying the stories of scripture, is a helpful tool for get-ting a fresh perspective on your own story, especially the formative incidents in your early life that shaped your sense of brokenness. Using the practice of *Lectio Divina* can help you transform your story from a source of pain to a source of understanding.

4. *Find meaning in your brokenness:* The Muslim practice of *hajj*, making a once-in-a-lifetime pilgrimage to a holy site, can be a literal or a virtual journey to a place that is sacred for you or to a key place where your story devel-oped. Returning with "new eyes" can help you find the meaning in your experience.

5. *Move on with your brokenness:* The ancient practice of walking a labyrinth is a way of symbolically walking a path that represents your inward—then outward—journey. The physical movement becomes a spiritual reflection that can help you integrate and move on while you are mending, rather than postponing your life until you reach the goal of a "cure."

6. *Transcend your brokenness:* Hindus refer to creativity as a "yoga," or a pathway to the Transcendent, and explor-ing your personal tools for creative expression can help you cope with and transcend your sense of brokenness.

7. *Share your brokenness:* Buddhism offers what are called the "Three Jewels": Buddha (a figure to be revered and

emulated), Dharma (teachings or practices), and *Sangha* (community). It is this third spiritual gem that speaks most powerfully to brokenness: You are not alone. Connection with a community to support you, and that you can support, is both a central core and a great comfort in your mending.

These teachings and practices from world religions have helped ease my suffering and aided my mending process, and I offer them to you in the pages of this book in the hope that if you feel spiritually, emotionally, mentally, or physically broken, you, too, will find some help. Whatever your faith tradition, I believe you will find kindness and wise counsel in this step-by-step process of recovering the wholeness you seek. You can do these practices at your own pace and in the order of your choosing. However, you may find it helpful to read through and practice the techniques in the order in which they are presented because I have found that most people benefit from this sequence. But don't feel bound by this order; you may find that not all of the techniques are helpful to you. You may want to dip into the book at any chapter to seek help with a particular problem. As you utilize these spiritual tools, it is my hope that you will find something in these pages to ease your pain and to help you find your hidden wholeness.

I do want to add one word of caution. If you begin with one of the practices and find yourself overwhelmed by dark thoughts and feelings, don't be afraid to seek the help of a therapist or spiritual advisor. There may be parts of your brokenness that you cannot mend on your own, and seeking help and support is a wise and kind thing to do for yourself. Also, refer to the next section titled "Emotional First Aid" for some suggestions for things you can do to cope with the feelings that might emerge.

As you will see throughout this book, brokenness has caused problems in my life (and probably in yours), but that same brokenness has also helped make me the person I am today. The challenge for me—and for you—is to hold both of those realities in tension within our hearts as we learn to cope and thrive just as we are.

The process of mending what is broken is a journey, not a destination. The journey you will undertake in this book is part of a lifelong process of recovering your true self. When you have finished this book, you probably won't be "healed," but you will be in possession of some new ways of looking at yourself and loving yourself ... even in your brokenness.

Emotional First Aid

BY FRANCES E. ENGLANDER, MA, ATR-BC, CPAT

Undertaking the readings and activities proposed in this book could be likened to undertaking a journey. When we prepare for a journey, we make an effort to pack what we anticipate needing to address our physical needs, and if we know the trip is going to take us someplace with potential hazards, we might pack a first aid kit. Likewise, as you embark on the journey in this book, it is important to pack what you anticipate needing to address your emotional needs and problems along the way.

Feelings of brokenness typically stem from aspects of your history that have been painful, traumatic, even overwhelming. As you revisit past experiences, it is not unusual to experience great swells of emotion. Many of the same feelings you had in the past may resurface in the present, and the most uncomfortable ones—fear, rage, grief, despair—can sometimes feel just as painful today as they did when you first experienced them. Here are some things you can do to prepare, and also to take care of yourself, should powerful feelings and dark thoughts emerge on your journey:

- First of all, know that this may happen and if it does, trust that it is a necessary part of the journey and one that need not be all-enveloping. Remember, you survived whatever circumstance you are remembering today, and that was *then*; this is *now*.

- You have undoubtedly already cultivated some strategies to manage your feelings. Take some time to be consciously aware of these. Which of them seem to be most helpful for you?

- Know your limits and respect them. What are your body's signals of being overwhelmed before you are overtaken? Does your heart race, your breathing grow rapid and shallow? Do you perspire or ache? Do your hands shake? Your face flush? When you tune in and notice such reactions, you can consciously stop, slow your breathing, and remove yourself to another setting, if need be.

- If you are feeling overwhelmed, consciously introduce a different sensory experience: smell a pleasant scent, touch or wrap yourself in something with a pleasing texture, treat yourself to delicious flavors, take a warm, soothing bath. Sometimes a benign but shocking sensory experience, such as putting an ice cube on your wrist, can help interrupt runaway feelings and return your attention to the here and now.

- Talk to someone—a trusted friend, relative, clergy person, counselor, therapist—someone you can depend on to listen and reassure you. As author Terry Taylor says, "When I found myself experiencing emotional reactions I couldn't control or understand, it led me to seek the assistance of a therapist who specializes in treatment of post-traumatic stress disorder." The key point is to recognize that there may be parts of your brokenness that you cannot mend without help from someone, preferably a professional in the mental health or spiritual direction field.

- Journal. Sometimes feelings translate more readily into scribbles and color. The words can come later. Having a journal you can open, close, and put safely away gives you the power to decide when, where, and how much of your memories and experiences you wish to address at a given time.

- Designate time limits. You can set a timer for a tolerable number of minutes, allowing yourself to feel and/or journal about difficult thoughts and emotions but promising yourself that when the timer beeps, you will focus on doing something else, preferably something fun or comforting.
- Say and/or write calming, reassuring things to yourself. Pray. Write affirmations of your goodness and safety. Treat yourself as someone you dearly love.

1

What Does It Mean to Be Broken?

An Encounter with Brokenness

I thought I knew everything there was to know about brokenness until the night of July 18, 2007, when I walked out a door and into a world in which my body and my life were shattered.

On that night, I was at Ghost Ranch, the Presbyterian Conference Center in northern New Mexico, where I was leading a weeklong workshop on world religions. Ironically, just the summer before I had led a workshop on "A Spirituality for Brokenness" at the same retreat center. I was no stranger to the subject of brokenness, personally or professionally. Over the preceding few years, I had led the brokenness workshop a number of times, and I had an array of advice and spiritual tools to offer to people who had a sense that their lives and spirits had somehow been shattered. I "knew" how to cope.

But on that night in July, the concept of brokenness was expanded for me dramatically and physically. I had just returned from taking the participants in my workshop on a visit to Dar al Islam Mosque, near the town of Abiquiu about fifteen minutes away. I was driving a van and had dropped off my passengers before heading back to my room in a small building called Ghost House. It was about 9:45 p.m. and already dark. When I got to Ghost House, I noticed that someone had left a light on in a public part of the building. Since there were signs all over campus asking visitors to turn off lights when leaving rooms, I walked in, switched off the light, and headed out the door.

As I stepped across the threshold, I apparently missed a step and did a swan dive onto my left shoulder and wrist. The pain that shot up and down my left arm was excruciating. I lay there for a moment, thinking about calling for help. Instead, somehow I managed to get to my feet and to the infirmary, only a few steps away. The nurse there recognized pretty quickly that I needed serious medical care, and he arranged for a Ghost Ranch staffer to drive me the thirty-five miles to the nearest hospital. I remember sitting slumped and crumpled beside the driver on the way to the hospital, repeating over and over that I wasn't sure I would be able to drive the next morning. (I was scheduled to take my group out to Christ in the Desert Monastery.) The driver must have thought I was crazy.

Tests at the hospital revealed that I had shattered my left shoulder and badly broken my wrist, and I was told that I needed surgery for a partial shoulder replacement and pins in my wrist. Unfortunately, no operating room was available until Friday morning, almost thirty-six hours later, so for the next day and a half, I sat up in bed (the only comfortable position I could find) in a heavily medicated state. I also discovered that I had badly bruised my right arm, and it was virtually impossible to get a telephone receiver to my ear or a cup, or even a straw, to my mouth.

I had a lot of time to think about the events leading up to my fall and about the different forms of brokenness I have experienced in my life.

THE ROOT OF BROKENNESS

My feeling of brokenness and unacceptability began within my immediate (and broken) family when I was taken away from my mother at age five and bounced from household to household and eventually abandoned by my mother altogether. My sense of brokenness was reconfirmed by my stepfamily. My stepmother told me constantly that I was too fat, that I was stupid and dirty, and my father's disinterest in me only added to my feeling of being unlovable. My mistaken beliefs were reinforced by my experiences in school, at church, with friends, in sports ... basically, everywhere I turned.

As I grew older, I found myself in a world that told me that if I wanted to "succeed," I would have to get ahead at any cost, win rather than cooperate, and measure my progress in terms of the number and monetary value of things I acquired. Listening to that siren song of our culture led me to bitterness, alcoholism, and an even greater sense of brokenness.

For many of us, our brokenness is deeply rooted in our childhood experiences and the painful adaptations we were forced to make simply in order to survive. Sadly, we also seem to learn our brokenness from friends, school, television, work, and sometimes even our religious institutions. Our world is itself shattered by war, hunger, disease, poverty, and—for much of the developed world—an obsession with materialism. The culture in which we live breaks us in many different ways. It tries to seduce us into becoming what we aren't (shallow and materialistic), into believing what we don't (that we can be happy only by acquiring more and more things), into acting in ways that we don't wish to (selfishly), and generally into accepting as "sane" a world that has observably gone over the edge (one in which we spend billions of dollars each year on weapons while people starve and go homeless in our midst). This advertising-saturated culture backs us into a corner where (if we have any feelings left at all) we feel alienated from the world, from each other, and, more critically, from ourselves.

Our brokenness expresses itself in a disconnect of mind from body, and body from spirit, and we have this uneasy sense that these aspects of our being are not in sync. Brokenness alters the very contours of our lives; it is life-changing, life-limiting. It is an almost indescribable feeling that there is something gravely wrong with us, something missing from our bodies or souls, a feeling that we are unacceptable to others and (worse) to ourselves; that we are, in a word, unlovable.

This feeling of brokenness is captured in the deeply insightful and compassionate words of Pema Chödrön, a Buddhist nun and one of my favorite spiritual teachers. She sums up the constellation of emotions that contribute to a feeling of brokenness by referring to them as "the embarrassment of being oneself." I can think of no better way to express the humiliation I sometimes feel.

When I first submitted the proposal for this book to my publisher, an editor asked me if "brokenness" was the right word for the problem I wanted to address; he wondered if "suffering" might be a better word. Without hesitation, I responded that "brokenness" was precisely the right word. Suffering might be a symptom of brokenness, but it is not the same thing. People suffer for a variety of reasons, such as grief, relationship problems, or illness, but brokenness is more than these things. Brokenness is more than a temporary emotion, more than a set of unfortunate circumstances. Brokenness is a *felt* state of being. People can feel broken whether or not they actually are. In spite of this, the feeling of brokenness is its own reality that must be acknowledged and honored.

I think this is something of what philosopher William James captured in his description of brokenness as "torn-to-pieces-hood": "We have all known that experience, for to be human *is* to feel at times divided, fractured, pulled in a dozen directions ... and to yearn for serenity, for some mending of our 'torn-to-pieces-hood.'"

This story of brokenness isn't just mine. It's the story of many people. It may be your story. We each have broken areas of our lives, whether from things that have happened to us or as consequences of our own choices. We each have times and situations where our very souls feel fractured. And whatever our individual physical, mental, or emotional brokenness, our sense of disconnect is almost always amplified by our Western culture that covers our eyes with a veil of illusion about what we "should" be.

Yet, ironically, it is our very attempt to cover up our flaws, to try to be what we "should," that prevents us from accepting who we really are *at our core*. Learning to see our brokenness for what it is is the first step on the journey toward wholeness.

MENDING, NOT HEALING

I have come to the paradoxical conclusion that if we are ever going to accept ourselves and move on with our lives, it is essential that we abandon the false hope that we will be "healed." In fact, when I begin my workshops on brokenness, one of the first things I say to the participants is, "I don't want to offend your religious sensibilities, but no one is going to show up and heal you. No one is going to save you. We ourselves are going to have to find a way to *live* with our brokenness."

Some months ago I was having coffee with my friend Joe, and he was telling me about his experience of visiting Rwanda, the site of one of the world's most horrifying genocides. He reached into his pocket and pulled out a gift for me—a small black bowl, about half the size of a coffee saucer. This bowl had been resurrected, phoenixlike, from the ashes of a building that had been burned down during the Rwandan holocaust. It had been lovingly created by a craftsman in a nontraditional way that made it prone to breakage and crumbling. As Joe put it into my hand, he apologized for the fact that a triangular piece of its lip was missing.

The moment the bowl touched my hand, I had a revelation that helped me see a core truth about brokenness: this bowl was broken and literally incomplete, but it was still recognizably a bowl. In that instant, I understood that, whether or not I am broken, I am still a person, and a *whole* person at that, and still lovable.

Think about it. If we stopped focusing all our energy on trying to "fix" ourselves, perhaps we could see that we are whole in spite of our brokenness ... or perhaps *because* of it! If we could stop our obsessive and pointless quest for a cure, we could begin to look at tools to help us accept and live with ourselves, just the way we are. If we could realize that *how* we are is not *who* we are, we could stop torturing ourselves with how we think things ought to be and, instead, make peace with how things really are. We could give up the illusion that we have control over our lives and the circumstances in which we live. Ironically, this surrender could help us begin the process of genuine mending. We could start recuperating. We could accept the fact that the end point of our mending may still leave scars—some visible to the world, some visible only to ourselves. We might realize that no matter what limitations our brokenness ties us to, we can find ways to adapt so that we can achieve many of our goals.

I think that hope for a cure, or for what some people call "healing," is often an illusion, especially when the word "healing" is taken to mean being restored to the way we were before we were broken. Over the years, I have come to believe that my body and my spirit are not going to be restored fully to the way they were before my traumatic childhood experience. Believing that I could somehow overcome "once and for all" the things that happened to me led me to try any number of methods that failed and, in some cases, left me worse off than before I began. Ultimately, these strategies boiled down to a fundamental attempt to deny that my experiences ever happened and to hide my scars because I was ashamed of them.

Paradoxically, it was when I accepted that I could not change what had happened to me that I began to experience some freedom from those experiences. I didn't discover *healing*, but I did discover that my life could be *mended*. I still bear some stitches and scars that won't go away, just as surgery scars remain from the tumble I took in New Mexico. Yet, when I could accept my brokenness, I was able to get out of a world of denial. What lay before me was the road to mending.

I believe you can transform your feeling of brokenness into something better and deeper than "healed." When you begin to understand what brokenness means, you will be armed with information that empowers you to take the steps that can turn your leaden feelings into opportunities for health and happiness. When you can accept (and perhaps even celebrate) your brokenness, you can cease your endless search for "healing" and get on with your life, scars and all.

Just before I arrived at Ghost Ranch, I had a phone conversation with my editor about this book. I was feeling that the writing process was not going well. Despite his reassurances, I still had a lingering feeling that there was something wrong with what I was writing. It just didn't sound like me. It sounded like me *trying* to impersonate someone writing a book about brokenness. Moreover, there was something in me that told me that I wasn't being as honest as I could be in the advice and tools that I offered.

As I lay in bed in the hospital with my broken body, I realized what the problem was: I had lost the immediacy of what being broken really meant. I had begun to deal with it in my writing in religious jargon rather than spiritual realities and, in so doing, had lost the connection to the very real (and for me, right then, very physical) pain that brokenness brings.

I remembered a story I had read about the spiritual master Ram Dass, author of the pioneering book *Be Here Now* that served as a spiritual road map for millions of young people in the 1970s (myself included). One night in February 1997, when Ram Dass was in his mid-sixties, he reached to answer a ringing telephone and collapsed. It turned out he was having a major stroke. He recovered, but in the film *Ram Dass: Fierce Grace* he described how, when he got to the hospital and was lying on a gurney looking up at the pipes in the emergency room ceiling, he realized that he was facing death and that he—this spiritual inspiration to an entire generation—*was terrified.* He stated that he didn't have a single spiritual thought. Here he was, "Mr. Spiritual," and he didn't orient toward the spirit. This catastrophic physical event was a spiritual test, and he said, flatly, "I flunked."

I felt very much that way as I lay in the hospital. All of my spirituality, and all of the advice and tools that I had offered to those who attended my workshops, seemed unavailable to me. My accident served as a catalyst to remind myself, and to encourage you, to discover the immediacy and effectiveness of spiritual tools for yourself. Practices, methods, and techniques are effective only if they are effective for *you!* The tools I offer on the pages of this book are not theoretical constructs to undertake because you feel as if you *should.* Rather, they are practical ways you can explore to find what helps you encounter your brokenness on your own terms, to find some easing of your suffering, and to begin taking steps toward mending.

Your unique spirituality of brokenness will emerge as you take this spiritual journey. Don't overthink it. Don't *try* too hard. Let go and trust the experience itself. Remember, the process of mending is a lifelong journey, not a one-stop destination, of recovering your complete self.

The Long, Perfect Loveliness of You

There's a wonderful twentieth-century poet named Galway Kinnell who wrote an elegant poem titled "St. Francis and the Sow" about a pig. One of the most beautiful lines is the gentle admonition that "sometimes it is necessary to reteach a thing its loveliness." With a grace that only master poets can muster, Kinnell describes St. Francis touching the forehead of a sow, telling her that she is lovely. The sow begins to remember this, all the way from her snout to the curl of her tail, down "through the great broken heart." Before our eyes, a beast that we usually dismiss as ugly and unworthy (just as we might dismiss ourselves) remembers "the long, perfect loveliness of sow." Kinnell poignantly reminds us that all things, even the seemingly unacceptable, have their own intrinsic beauty and value.

Sometimes we, like the sow, forget how wonderful we really are. Perhaps we should stop expending so much energy trying to fix ourselves and, instead, spend more time considering our own "long, perfect loveliness."

I am reminded once again of the crumbly little bowl that Joe gave me, created, literally, out of the ashes of hate. I could choose to see what's missing from it, or to view it as just a few shattered pieces hanging together, a reminder of tragedy and brokenness. But as I look at it on my altar each morning, I see that its missing piece isn't a flaw. It gives this bowl a unique character. In fact, if it weren't for the small missing piece, I'm not sure I would ever look at this small piece of otherwise unremarkable clay. Its brokenness is not hidden, but rather reveals much more of its true "self." I think this is accurate for us as well. As we get closer to our true selves, we get closer to our core beauty, to a direct experience of the Transcendent not as "out there" somewhere, but within us.

2

SABBATH

Recognizing Your Brokenness

THE MOST IMPORTANT STEP: DOING NOTHING

The most important thing you can do to face your brokenness is … nothing. I'm not kidding. Doing "nothing" is actually doing something very important. Doing nothing gives you the opportunity to sit down and create a space where anything can happen.

If you are like me, you have tried anything and everything to heal yourself. Over the years, I have read hundreds of books, listened to scores of tapes, and attended dozens of workshops, each proclaiming that its road to healing was the one and only way that would work. I seemed to be always looking for "the next new thing," a meditation technique, a prayer practice, a journaling approach that would make me feel normal and unblemished. For much of my adult life, I have been searching for what I call a "light switch solution," something that I could do right now that would change my life dramatically and instantaneously. I haven't found it yet. I don't think I ever will.

Step one on the journey to mending brokenness is to cease the process of torturing ourselves with self-help. We need to stop trying to fix ourselves and take time to just do nothing so that we can get in touch with who we really are.

Not long after I returned home from my surgery in New Mexico, I found myself in a foul mood and in conflict with my partner, Fran. I felt she didn't understand what I was going through. She wisely decided to go shopping for a while to let me stew in my own resentment, and it turns out that time alone was precisely what I needed. It enabled me—perhaps for the first time since my accident—to face what had happened to me on that threshold at Ghost Ranch. During the hours Fran was gone, a change came over me. I can't explain it, other than to say that the very act of beholding my anger and resentment helped defuse it. By the time Fran returned, my mood had changed dramatically for the better. The man she had left snarling and sarcastic was now gentle and appreciative.

The shift came about at least in part because I had taken time to stop and consider with both my head and my heart what was going on. Stopping was the most important thing I did—and that points to the significance of perhaps the most important tool I have found to help in the mending process: taking a Sabbath experience.

Actually, I suggest taking *three* kinds of Sabbath—a daily, a weekly, and a semiannual Sabbath—but, in fact, any amount of time spent in intentional rest and reflection can be beneficial. Even a Sabbath-on-demand. Anything that "makes spacious what is cramped … makes large out of small, generous out of stingy, simple out of complex, choice out of obligation," as Donna Schaper, senior minister at Judson Memorial Church in New York City, describes it in her book *Sabbath Sense: A Spiritual Antidote for the Overworked.*

But when the time comes to slow down the pace and spend time in reflection, it's not easy to know where to start. After all, our culture is not one to place a high priority on taking the time to do nothing. Fortunately, we do have at our disposal a ready-made model for intentionally setting aside time for spiritual reflection: the Jewish and Christian tradition of the

Sabbath. Before I move on to talk about *how* to do nothing, I want to take a few moments to consider this idea of Sabbath, its meaning, and how it can be important in helping you deal with your sense of brokenness.

GETTING AWAY FROM THE SCREECH OF DISSONANT DAYS

Taking a Sabbath, a regular period of rest and reflection, is a tradition in both the Jewish and Christian faiths, and one of the Ten Commandments of the Hebrew Bible: "Remember the Sabbath day and keep it holy. For six days you shall labor and do all your work. But the seventh day is a Sabbath to the Lord your God; you shall not do any work" (Exodus 20:8–10).

Sabbath (from the Hebrew word "shabbat") means, literally, "to rest," and the traditional way of resting is to cease working for a day to reflect on creation and rejoice in it, and to consider what we have done in the previous week. In his celebrated classic *The Sabbath*, Abraham Joshua Heschel, leading theologian and religious philosopher, wrote that to keep the Sabbath is to "set apart one day a week for freedom," to "go away from the screech of dissonant days, from the nervousness and fury of acquisitiveness and the betrayal in embezzling [our] own life."

Yet the idea of taking one day out of seven to rest and refresh ourselves may be the commandment that is most often ignored by almost everyone except the most observant Jews and Christians. In ignoring this commandment (which is actually more of a gift than a demand) to take a Sabbath, many of us treat ourselves like machines that must be working constantly in order to make income or accomplish something. We don't even give ourselves the break that factory operators give their machines for periodic maintenance!

Unfortunately, the idea of keeping the Sabbath may bring up unpleasant memories for some of us. In the household where I grew up, Sabbath came loaded down with so many rules and regulations that I couldn't enjoy it. On Sabbath days, I felt separated from the things, such as play, that made me happy. It wasn't the idea of keeping the Sabbath that was the problem, it was the way my parents forced me to practice it.

I have finally been able to rediscover Sabbath and the joy it can bring. I've learned that Sabbath-keeping can be fun and, moreover, have a profound impact on my life by reducing stress and anxiety, and refreshing me. But first I had to learn what it truly meant to stop.

THE BENEFITS OF DOING NOTHING

Doing nothing means to stop doing anything that feels like a task. Anything that feels like work. Doing nothing is a gift. Every opportunity to do nothing is a sabbatical from the addictive and poisonous culture of busyness in which we live.

But, the truth is, we don't do "nothing" well. Western culture tends to frown on people who do nothing. In *Sabbath Sense: A Spiritual Antidote for the Overworked*, Donna Schaper humorously, but all too accurately, points out that we even work at taking vacations—planning, trying to make them "perfect," bringing our "connections" that keep us attached to busyness right along with us.

Yet creating a Sabbath experience of "doing nothing" may well be the most important step you can take in mending your brokenness. If you just *stop*, you give yourself a chance to give up the fruitless effort to find a cure for what ails you, and you suddenly have time to spend with yourself, just as you are.

As I've worked with people who are struggling with brokenness, one of the biggest obstacles I see is that they don't allow themselves the time they need to let themselves mend. We need to remember that broken bones will mend if supported and given time. Sometimes we argue that we can't stop because our lives keep us too busy, but other times I think we (I include myself in this) keep our lives busy (consciously or unconsciously) because it is simpler to keep moving than to slow down and face our brokenness in a still and silent place.

In adopting a Sabbath practice, you will be giving yourself the opportunity to remove yourself (at least for a regular period of time) from constant pressure and stress so you can reflect on what you are experiencing in your life. If this sounds ominous or threatening, be reassured that I'm not proposing a you've-got-to-face-it confrontation with your problems, but rather a gentle Sabbath stillness that will allow you to connect with your compassionate, inner observer. Sabbath is time set apart when you can suspend judgment about your situation and see yourself more clearly. It is a period of intentional inactivity that can give you the downtime you need to help you recognize your pain and, ultimately, befriend it.

Sabbath-keeping can free you up to encounter your brokenness on its own terms. At the same time, it can give you time to refresh yourself periodically so you have the strength to undertake the practices that can help you mend. By removing from the Sabbath anything that counts as a task, and keeping only those things that please and refresh you, your Sabbath periods will open up spaces in which you can experience gratefulness for the joys in your life. Your Sabbaths will become something to look forward to, something to savor.

What might it be like for you if you could look at your life and your work and realize that they are not complete until you learn to do *nothing* for at least a small period of time—each day, each week, and periodically during the year?

TAKING A DAILY SABBATH

In the original meaning of Sabbath, the holy time recurs once a week, but when it comes to mending, I highly recommend taking some Sabbath time *every day* to do nothing. And when I talk about just doing *nothing*, I mean it.

If you're thinking "every day" is a bit much, I can only tell you that this quiet experience has made my days more livable and, with practice, less difficult and less uncomfortable. Sitting in silence, doing nothing has palpably changed the quality of my days. On the days when I meditate, I feel more relaxed. There is less tension in my face. I sleep better. I find it easier to cope with people I might normally find annoying. My thinking is more focused. I feel more creative.

You can take a mini-Sabbath by just sitting still, without using any formal meditation techniques. I particularly suggest beginning without using any formal meditation techniques because techniques often come saddled with a need to be competitive and hierarchical. They can cause you to begin asking yourself if you are using the "best" technique, if you are meditating long enough (or short enough), and if you are doing it "right." If there are rules and you don't follow them, you may feel as if you have failed, and that will just add to your pain.

Most days, I sit in silence for about twenty minutes in the early morning. Sometimes my little dog, Jusqu'a, joins me. But don't take my practice of twenty minutes a day as a rule or a demand; start out with an amount of time that feels comfortable for you. Five or ten minutes will do. The important thing is to do nothing for some period of time *every day* (including the weekend).

While there are no rules for your mini-Sabbath, it is important to consider *where* you will take your quiet time. This is almost as important as the act of doing nothing itself. Think of your location as your sacred space. Try to find a spot that affords opportunities for silence and solitude, a place that you can reserve to yourself, that is not accessible to others. It should be in a low traffic area, preferably one where your spouse, partner, children, parents, business associates, or classmates (essentially, everyone in your world) will leave you alone. You might be able to arrange for a place that is beautiful, or your sacred space might be as simple as a bedroom that can be locked, or even a bathroom. One friend of mine set up a sacred space in her closet. Whatever spot you choose, try to find a location that delivers the minimum number of visual distractions and maximum amount of silence.

By silence, I mean the absence of unnatural sounds. I also mean the absence of human voices. Once you remove these distractions from your sacred space, you can focus on calming your spirit. You can begin to turn down the noise in your head. You can learn to savor silence. You can relearn the ability to replace human-created music with the sound of wind and the rustle of leaves. You can begin to hear the chirping speech of birds. You can rediscover the muffled sounds of your breathing and your heartbeat.

I also want to add a word about "visual noise." For me, pictures or decorations tend to be distracting, so I find it helpful to sit facing a blank wall. You may find that, as pleasant as looking out a window is, the view can draw your attention away from yourself to whatever is happening outside. Or, if you sit facing into a room, your eyes may focus on items or work that need your attention. Facing a blank wall is a matter of personal preference, so I suggest you experiment to see what best works for you. When all of the subtractions of unnatural sound and sight are added up, they total an experience where you can be alone and quiet, where you can learn to take a long, loving look at yourself.

One element that can make your sacred space more meaningful is an altar. I'm not talking about the kind of altar that is connected with a particular religion, but rather something that offers a symbolic way of honoring your space, of reflecting your thoughts and feelings.

In my small apartment, I have created an altar space in an area adjacent to my dining room where I have placed a small black table against the wall. The table is an antique, nearly two hundred years old, black, and without artifice or decoration. Its flat top is about waist high for me. On top of the table I have placed a simple, Zen-style, two-tier candleholder and the broken black bowl from Rwanda, which serves as a symbol of my brokenness. The table has one drawer where I keep various religious and spiritual objects that I have acquired over the years, such as a religious medal of St. Thomas the Apostle (the doubting Thomas), stones I have picked up at Ghost Ranch and other locations that hold deep meaning for me, a feather, incense, a rosary, a prayer card, and a relic of St. Gemma. Depending on my emotional or spiritual mood, I sometimes reach into this drawer for things to place on top of my altar.

If you want to create an altar for yourself, it can be as simple or as elaborate as you wish. You may want to collect items that have particular meaning for you and add them to your space as you move through your mending journey. I have only two suggestions to make: one, that you allow for maximum flexibility so you can change your altar in a variety of ways to suit your spiritual needs; and, two, if your altar is in a spot where others can pass by and see it, clarify that this is *your* space, and that it is important to you, and ask others to respect what you have created.

Once you have designated your sacred space, take a few moments to consider how you will use it:

- Consider *when* you will take your Sabbath time. You might want to do it first thing in the morning, when it is still dark, before others in the household are up. Or, perhaps late in the evening after work and family responsibilities have wound down for the day. Remember, I'm not talking about a long period of time; even a few minutes of silence, a short time of doing nothing, can make a difference.
- Consider *how* you will quiet yourself. You might want to perform a small ritual of your own creation to mark your movement from "ordinary" time to sacred silent time, such as simply lighting a candle.
- Consider *how long* you will give yourself the gift of Sabbath. You might want to set a timer to signal when your time is up, so you can let go of thoughts about the passage of time for the duration of your quiet. When the timer beeps, reset it if you feel you need more time. Remember, this time of "doing nothing" is a gift you are giving to yourself, not another "to do" on your list for the day.

A Word of Caution

If you are not used to spending time in silence and solitude, you may initially find the experience of doing nothing to be, literally, painful. This is especially true with time spent in silent meditation.

Some years ago, I had the opportunity to spend two weeks in an Episcopal monastery in lower Michigan, trying out the monastic life, living and working side by side with the monks, following their daily routine.

One part of the daily schedule called for us to each spend half an hour in silent prayer once a day, just before supper. We were told that we could go anywhere we liked on the grounds of the monastery as long as we found a place where we could be alone and where we would be silent.

The first afternoon I did this, I found myself in extreme emotional pain almost from the moment I got settled. I had chosen to sit in the church. It was a warm summer day, and the church did not have air conditioning, so the distant natural sounds that seeped in from outside the doors and windows were the only sounds around me.

I was unprepared for the inrush of "noise" from negative self-talk that commenced the moment I settled into one of the pews. My inner voice instantly started telling me that I was different from everybody else. That I wasn't as good as everybody else. That I was unacceptable to others (and myself). That I was, to put it simply, unlovable. Prior to this, I don't think I had ever sat in silence for more than a minute or two in my whole life. In fact, I used every kind of external noise and stimulation I could find to drown out the inner pain I felt.

At first, sitting in silence confirmed for me why I didn't like silence or solitude. Who would want to sit in silence and aloneness when that meant subjecting yourself to emotional pain? But I decided to tough it out, and I'm glad that I did. It helped me see for the first time what I was running away from: my lifelong habit of verbal self-abuse whenever my mind wasn't focused on something else.

My pain continued through that first half hour, and again the next afternoon, but I was finally beginning to see what was going on. By the third day, my mind was beginning to quiet down, and my emotional pain lessened in severity. After a few days, the anguish left me, and I began to look forward to the daily period of silent prayer as a gift. Today, whether I am at my altar at home in the early morning darkness or in a hotel if I am traveling, I always look forward to my portion of silence and solitude. In a surprising turnaround, I also can feel a difference in my daily routine if I haven't had my quiet time; without it, I find noise, discomfort, and irritation in what I am doing.

As you allow yourself to enter the quiet, you may find yourself feeling overwhelmed by dark thoughts and feelings. Please don't be afraid to seek the help of a therapist or spiritual advisor. Remember that pain shared is half the pain. But I also urge you to stick with your sitting in silence, even if it is painful at first. Whether you begin your day or end it with a period of silence and solitude, you will find yourself refreshed, more focused, and ready to meet the challenges that each day presents. These benefits may not begin to show themselves immediately, but if you are patient, you may find yourself beginning to look forward to each day's time of doing nothing. For me, it is my favorite time of the day. There's another benefit as well: when you begin to take time to do nothing for a period of time each day, you gain the opportunity not only to come face to face with your brokenness but also to recognize your hidden wholeness.

TAKING A WEEKLY SABBATH

As you begin to feel comfortable taking a daily time to do nothing, I recommend working toward some kind of weekly Sabbath experience of doing nothing that counts as a task for at least several hours. Your Sabbath doesn't necessarily have to fall on a Saturday or Sunday; it can be any day you choose. It doesn't have to be a full twenty-four-hour period; that may not be possible. It might be possible for you to take a morning, an afternoon, or an evening for yourself. If that's too much, try hanging a "do not disturb" sign on your life for an hour or two once a week. The experience of this weekly sabbatical is palpably different from that of a daily meditation period. It is time to do what refreshes you, a time to enjoy the benefits of play.

Just recently, I started taking a half-day Sabbath on Saturday mornings, from the time I get up until noon. Actually, my Sabbath begins on Friday night when I go to bed. I only have one rule for myself about Saturday mornings: I don't do anything that would count as a task. I don't read or send e-mails, clean up the kitchen, respond to phone messages, or do anything related to my work. I limit myself to doing things that I enjoy and that are relaxing and refreshing. I like to cook, so I usually prepare breakfast for myself (buttermilk pancakes from scratch!). I also like to read, watch movies, and listen to music. Sometimes I just sit and reflect on what has transpired during the previous six days.

I actively protect this time. I am not afraid to tell friends and business colleagues that this is my Sabbath. They respect that and leave me alone on Saturday mornings. And when the unavoidable conflict does come up (and it does), I make sure that I take a morning on another day of the week for my Sabbath.

My weekly Sabbath is different from my daily meditation period. I still subtract the painful and annoying and distracting things in my life, but rather than sitting silently and in solitude, I refresh myself by spending time doing the things I like to do, the things I want to do, the things I choose to do.

I will share this word of warning out of my experience: Whether it's your daily meditation experience or your weekly Sabbath, temptations will immediately present themselves. Be wary of them. The first Saturday on which I kept a Sabbath, I woke up and told myself that maybe I could just check my e-mails for a minute. It was surprisingly hard to resist, but I did!

Here are some suggestions to consider as you think about how you might enjoy your weekly Sabbath:

- Make a list of the things you *don't like* to do and post it; avoid doing anything on that list during your Sabbath time.
- Make a list of things you *like* to do; choose from this list on your Sabbath.
- Planning your Sabbath time may be useful, but I also suggest starting your Sabbath with no plan and seeing what happens.
- When you reach the end of your Sabbath time, savor the moment; reflect on how you have spent your time. What was it about the experience that brought you joy? Also reflect on the things you want to be thankful for.
- Journal about your Sabbath time, but with this caveat: if journaling feels like a task, journal after your Sabbath ends.
- If no task is urgently demanding your attention when your Sabbath time ends, why not extend it for a few hours?

TAKING A LONGER SABBATICAL

Finally, I recommend that you expand your Sabbath time to an entire weekend every few months. I can already hear you saying, "That won't happen, there's too much to do, it's too expensive," and so on. But I am talking about an important piece of your mending, and I urge you not to dismiss this suggestion. Getting out of your house or apartment for a retreat, for example, at some kind of retreat or conference center in a wooded setting is a good idea and is usually not very expensive.

I've found that getting away to a different location is particularly refreshing, especially if you can do something you can't do at home: ski, go surfing, climb a mountain, go scuba diving (even if it's in a swimming pool), or climb a tree. By all means, avoid places and things that feel like work, such as computer rooms at hotels, conference centers, any place that seems to invite you to perform a task. You might visit a friend you haven't seen for years. Or perhaps you might even do something that feels a little out of your comfort zone—nothing too dangerous or threatening, just enough to be a bit of a challenge and shift you out of your daily routines.

Any place or activity that will shift you out of the ordinary and bring you rest and a sense of pleasure is good. If you can't "get away," don't abandon the idea of taking a longer Sabbath. Look around with creative eyes. What interests you? Here are some suggestions to stimulate your thinking:

- Go someplace local you have always wanted to visit but haven't
- Do something you haven't done before
- Sleep late, or get up early
- Try some unusual foods that would not normally be part of your diet
- Visit a house of worship for a religion other than your own

Taking a longer time to rest and restore yourself is just as important as a daily quiet time or a weekly time to do nothing. Remember, even industries give their machines "downtime" for periodic maintenance. Without such times, we grow weary, stressed, and irritable. When I don't take this periodic extended Sabbath time, I feel run-down. People around me can tell.

You can certainly choose to take any of these Sabbath opportunities—daily, weekly, periodically—or none at all. But if you try to work the three different periods of "Sabbath time" together, you may discover that you have created a very powerful ritual rhythm in your life. Knowing that you have a break coming up every week, and a more significant break periodically, is energizing. Once you set up this three-part rhythm, respect it just as you would a regular schedule of business meetings and reports. Your downtime is not a lark; it is an integral part of mending your brokenness.

The point of doing nothing is to stop trying to fix yourself, and when you have taken that step, you have already accomplished a great deal. Taking time for daily, weekly, and periodic Sabbath time offers even more benefits. First, there is the healing property of rest that such time provides. Doing nothing frees up space in your schedule for the mending that your body, mind, and spirit need. The second benefit is the opportunity to just spend time with yourself, to feel self-acceptance, to discover the hidden wholeness that lies within your brokenness. Third, the three periods of rest work together to establish a rhythm of relaxation and re-creation that can become part of your spiritual practice. Finally, taking time on a regular basis to do nothing sets the stage for you to embark on an exploration of other spiritual tools, which we will explore in the chapters ahead, that can help you mend.

3

MAITRI AND TONGLEN
Having Compassion for Your Brokenness

WHEN YOU DO NOTHING, DARK THINGS BEGIN TO APPEAR

Once you have stopped trying to fix yourself and have begun to take daily and weekly (and maybe quarterly) Sabbath times to do nothing, you might begin to encounter more directly the emotional pain of "the embarrassment of being you." When I first heard Pema Chödrön describe this, I laughed out loud because her words expressed exactly the embarrassment I felt about my brokenness—and why I have always tried to hide it. Why, when I take time in silence and just do nothing, dark ideas begin to creep into my consciousness. Why I often intentionally fill my days with people and noise to drown out the emotional pain I feel when I am left to myself.

For many of us who feel broken, one of the most troubling aspects of our condition is that we feel different from other people, unworthy, not acceptable. There is likely to be a sense of shame involved. Because we tend to internalize our feeling of brokenness and make it part of our identity, our sense of shame isn't limited to whatever we are feeling broken about. Instead, we generalize our feeling of embarrassment to our entire being. In other words, we don't necessarily feel embarrassed about our brokenness, we feel embarrassed at being *ourselves*!

When we "let down our guard," with nothing to fill up the space, we may come face to face with the emotional pain that often lurks just beneath the surface of our consciousness. This pain is often rooted in the very core of our brokenness and is often clever and tenacious in its hold over us. Because of that, it is important that we acquire some tools to deal with the "emotional sludge" that can ooze up in times of silence or meditation.

I first encountered the interconnected Tibetan Buddhist meditation techniques of *maitri* (MY-tree) and *tonglen* (tong-len) in the teachings of Pema Chödrön, and I immediately knew I had found two spiritual tools that could be immensely helpful in easing my anguish. Both techniques are built on the idea of compassion: *maitri*, on compassion for ourselves, and *tonglen*, on compassion for other people who are hurting in the same way we are. *Maitri* is a Sanskrit word meaning compassion, or more literally, "unconditional friendship with oneself," and *tonglen* is a means of using personal suffering to awaken compassion for others. Both have significant implications for working with brokenness, and I am indebted to Pema for her insights.

MAKING FRIENDS WITH YOURSELF

The term *maitri* is used in two different ways. First and foremost, it describes an attitude or spirit of friendliness that you can bring to yourself—your emotional life, your memories, even your very body. Pema calls it a fundamental attitude of nonaggression. Or, to put it another way, it is the mindset of being sympathetic to yourself, without harshness. *Maitri* is also a specific meditation process in the Tibetan Buddhist tradition through which you can develop this feeling of unconditional friendliness toward yourself—and, I would add, toward your brokenness. I'll explore this in more depth in a minute, but first it's important to grasp how this idea of "befriending yourself" might be a significant spiritual tool for mending your brokenness.

When was the last time you felt relaxed with yourself? Satisfied with who you are? At home with yourself? A friend to yourself? All these are encompassed in the term *maitri*. The idea of learning to feel friendly toward yourself might sound odd at first, but—be honest now—it is probably not something you practice when you are feeling broken. Instead, you probably are far more likely to criticize yourself, or be angry with yourself, or dwell in the depression and shame of "being yourself." Though learning to be friendly toward your pain might sound like a paltry response at first, it is, in fact, a powerful step toward mending your brokenness.

Think about it: if your best friend were feeling anguished or embarrassed, you would offer what any good friend would offer— words of affirmation and love, accompanied by a dose of reality. You certainly wouldn't condemn your friend or tell him or her to "get over it." It is essentially the same process in befriending your- self through *maitri*. You look at your pain the way a close friend would. Or better yet, you look at your misery in the same way you would look at the pain your best friend was feeling. You see your pain through the eyes of compassion rather than criticism or judgment. You are willing to stay with your pain, to befriend it. This is when change can begin. Healthy change. The kind of change that can put you on the road to mending.

Allowing yourself to feel your pain, to really acknowledge its presence, and adopting an attitude of compassion toward yourself can have remarkably positive effects in your life. As Pema points out in *When Things Fall Apart: Heart Advice for Difficult Times,* "A thoroughly good relationship with ourselves results in our being still, which doesn't mean we don't run and jump and dance about. It means there's no compulsiveness. We don't overwork, overeat, oversmoke, overseduce. In short, we begin to stop causing harm."

I experienced the benefits of *maitri* compassion firsthand during the aftermath of my arm injury. Originally, the surgeon in

New Mexico had told me that my arm would be in a cast for about six weeks. Somehow, in my self-delusion, I had thought that when the cast came off, I would be as good as new, able to move about and work as though nothing had happened. But the reality was quite different. When the cast came off, it became apparent that I had developed reflex sympathetic dystrophy (RSD), a syndrome that leaves the hand on the affected side swollen and stiff, a condition that can be permanent.

My first reaction to this diagnosis was more anger and resentment, but practicing *maitri* helped me come to a place of equanimity about my condition, even as I worked to improve it. Through *maitri*, I came to see my pain and brokenness not as an invader but as a friend that brought its own set of special gifts, such as a sense of appreciation for others who suffer, and a sense of gratitude for the health and wholeness of the rest of me.

I think it is much the same with emotional injuries. We want to believe that some healing aid will "cure" us, make us "good as new," yet we're frustrated when the same old hurts or depressions or angers seem to keep plaguing us. The practice of *maitri* invites us to look at our pain—whether physical injuries or emotional memories—not as something to be avoided but as something to be embraced, to be tended, to feel kindly toward. *Maitri* teaches us that our woundedness presents us with an opportunity to begin to care for ourselves in the fullest sense, with compassion for the depth of our anguish, what it is about, and where it is coming from.

In *When Things Fall Apart*, Pema also makes the observation, which I recognize only too well, that our first impulse is usually to flee, rather than face, what is painful or difficult. *Maitri* is deliciously counterintuitive. Instead of offering escape, *maitri* brings us face to face with our demons. *Maitri* gives us the opportunity to look deeply at our brokenness with—*and this is the key*—lovingkindness. *Maitri* gives us the time and space we need to come to terms, through grieving, with the fact that returning to a state of wholeness (healing) may not be a viable option for us.

Paradoxically, adopting this state of friendly acceptance of our brokenness is, instead of being a stance of defeat, precisely the stance that can bring us one step closer to mending. As Pema says on her DVD *Good Medicine: How to Turn Pain into Compassion with* Tonglen *Meditation,* "Moving closer to your experience instead of trying to run away from it becomes the basis of really being able to open your heart to a multitude of situations, a multitude of people which now seem impossible to open your heart to."

With the practice of *maitri,* you can stop avoiding the difficult things in your life and begin to feel empathy for your pain. You can also learn to get control of the negative behaviors that stem from not acknowledging your pain. You can stop blaming others for your problems. You can stop flying off the handle at loved ones. When you stop burying your anguish, you can let go of the ways you might try to self-medicate your pain through overeating or starving, abusing alcohol or drugs, smoking, over-exercising, overworking—whatever your self-destructive coping mechanism is. When you stop trying to escape your pain, you are taking an important step toward an attitude of lovingkindness for your brokenness.

PREPARING TO PRACTICE

At the beginning of the workshops that I lead about brokenness, I usually ask the participants what coping mechanisms they are using to hide from their brokenness. I find that participants reveal a remarkable variety of (and sometimes very creative) coping mechanisms. The one thing they all have in common, however, is that most of the coping mechanisms I hear about involve ways of hiding from brokenness and its pain. The practice of *maitri* does just the opposite: Instead of immediately trying to get rid of pain, *maitri* invites us to lean into the pain and see what happens.

One recent summer when I was leading a weeklong program on "A Spirituality for Brokenness," I told the group that we would spend our first day and a half just sitting with our pain, writing about it, feeling it, giving it a name. One participant, a member of the clergy, complained very emphatically that she was fully aware of her pain, that she did not want to do this, and that she wanted to move on to the next step.

At my encouragement, she reluctantly agreed to proceed with the session, but at one point she felt such anguish that she got up and fled the room. I went after her and brought her back. This time, she was able to stay with her pain, and by the time we had worked through the entire weeklong process of coming to grips with the embarrassment of being ourselves and learning to love ourselves in spite of—I dare say *because* of—our brokenness, she had come to a point of spiritual acceptance about herself.

This beginning phase of *maitri* is perhaps the hardest. Allowing your bad memories even a *little* breathing room can feel threatening, even terrifying. If you feel broken, you can easily become overwhelmed by your pain. So before you begin a *maitri* practice, it will be important to know what you can do, and to whom you can go, if you do feel overwhelmed. (See "Emotional First Aid" at the beginning of the book for some suggestions.)

Here are a few more things you can do to help prepare for a rewarding *maitri* experience:

- Be open to just sitting quietly with yourself.
- Don't expect immediate results. Having compassion for yourself involves having patience and letting go of certain expectations.
- Make a commitment to practicing *maitri* on a regular schedule over an extended period of time (days, weeks, perhaps even months). Befriending your pain will probably take time, and it is important not to give up on yourself too early.
- Be as honest as you can with yourself about what you are feeling, especially the intensity of your pain. If it's a ten on a scale of one to ten, recognize that. But if it's a one or a two, be honest in noting that your pain isn't as severe as you expected it might be.

- Try to have a sense of humor about yourself and what you are going through. It might be helpful to remember that many comedy movies are built around characters going through disastrous events. Those events can be viewed as tragic or comic, depending on the attitude viewers adopt toward them.
- Embrace the idea of being compassionate toward yourself. Compassion doesn't mean pity; it means "to suffer with." Try to look at your situation the way that you would view the troubles of your closest friend if he or she were suffering.
- Avoid condemning yourself. You've probably already spent enough time beating yourself up.

THE PRACTICE OF *MAITRI*

Are you ready to give *maitri* a try? Here's a suggested step-by-step approach you can use, but keep in mind that these are only suggestions, not rules.

- Start by setting a specific length of time for your *maitri*. I use twenty minutes, but find a length of time that works for you ... then stick to it!
- If possible, find a place to meditate that is quiet and free from distractions.
- Either sit on the floor or on a mat in a comfortable position. Or, if you are like me (I have some problems with arthritis) and can't sit comfortably on the floor for extended periods of time, sit in a comfortable straight-back chair for support.
- Sit up straight. Don't slouch. If you're sitting on a chair, place the soles of your feet flat on the floor, with your feet a comfortable shoulder-width apart.
- Either fold your hands in your lap or place them palms down on your thighs.

- Sit facing a blank wall if possible.
- Either close your eyes or try to keep them half open and unfocused. You might also try focusing on a single point or object.
- Consciously relax all parts of your body step by step, beginning with your feet, moving on to your calves, and continuing upward until you have relaxed your face and head.
- Once you have relaxed, begin getting in touch with your feelings, especially your pain (physical or emotional).
- Note where you feel your pain and how strong it is.
- Try not to let your attention move away from your discomfort. If you find yourself thinking about something else, return your attention to your pain in the same way that you would return to repeating your mantra if you were practicing a form of mindfulness meditation.
- Start to think of your pain as a separate entity, a companion within yourself. Consider giving it a name so you can address it.
- Talk to your pain. Ask it questions: "Why are you with me? What do you need? Is there something that will make you go away? Do you want to go away? If not, is there something that will soothe you? Do you have something to tell me?"
- Listen for your pain's answers. These answers may not come as words, but in dreams, coincidences, or other psychological or emotional phenomena.
- Once you have begun thinking of your pain as a companion, try to think of it in a loving way, in the same way you would care about a troubled but lovable relative or partner.

It may not be easy to think of your pain in a loving way at first, but do give it time. *Maitri* can help you learn to look at your day-to-day life with honesty, humor, and compassion, not condoning or condemning, and it is well worth your time and effort to give it a try.

LEANING INTO THE PAIN

For many years I have been plagued with the grief of thinking that I did something at the age of eight that drove my mother away forever. During the quiet of my daily morning "do nothing" Sabbath times, that dark and inappropriate feeling of responsibility sometimes visits me. When this memory comes up, I don't try to change the subject in my internal conversation. Instead, I treat it like any other thought that might occur to me at that time and just let it drift by. Sometimes, that's all it takes, and the pain passes on its own accord.

But sometimes the pain remains. When it does, I make a mental note to come back to it in a *maitri* practice. If possible, I like to do the *maitri* later in the same day, when I can consciously sit with this anguish for a fixed period of time (usually ten or twenty minutes). If I tell myself that my pain is unbearable, I will begin to despair and may feel like giving up. But if I can gradually adopt an attitude of compassion and friendliness toward it, and myself, I can look for some creative ways to cope with my brokenness.

This process isn't easy at first, but after a while it does soften the pain. *Maitri* won't cure you overnight of your painful memories, your embarrassment, your self-loathing, or whatever painful form your brokenness takes. But *maitri* can ease your journey every step of the way. *Maitri* isn't an end in itself, but rather a step in the process of connecting with your own pain so you can live with it gently and help your wounds mend.

I recommend that you continue your daily time of Sabbath, but add to it a separate period every day or two to practice *maitri*. How often and how long you practice *maitri* depends on several factors: how you are doing in grieving over the fact that you may never again feel whole; how comfortable you are about accepting your brokenness; and how able you are to look at yourself, and especially your brokenness, with lovingkindness. This process may take days, weeks, months, or longer. But stay with it.

Once you have become comfortable with nurturing friendliness toward yourself and your sense of brokenness through the practice of *maitri*, you are ready to begin practicing *tonglen*, the Tibetan Buddhist practice of connecting your pain with the pain of others in a way that can make your suffering more bearable.

THE PRACTICE OF *TONGLEN*

For those of us who feel broken, one of the most disturbing delusions with which we torture ourselves is the idea that we are alone in our pain. In reality, there are thousands, if not millions, of people throughout the world who feel as pained and as unlovable as we do. It may surprise you to think of using your suffering to connect with others as a way of making your pain meaningful and, therefore, more manageable. Yet, as with *maitri*, there is a counterintuitive element in the meditative practice of *tonglen*: as you unite your pain with the pain of others, and understand that you are not alone, you can become more compassionate toward yourself, thereby further empowering your practice of *maitri*.

Picture a large circular motion, starting with *maitri* (a deep compassion for yourself and your brokenness), then moving through the meditative practice of *tonglen* (a sense of profound compassion for others), and coming back again to *maitri* with a richer, more meaningful sense of yourself in the "big picture." As Pema puts it, once you feel your pain "as something that will soften and purify" you, it will make you "far more loving and kind." Your pain and vulnerability are powerful places where you can connect with others, even take on the suffering of others, and send out joy and goodness. This, in turn, can help you overcome your own sense of isolation and loneliness, and ease your own pain.

The practice of *tonglen* can be complicated, but the basics are relatively straightforward. Usually it involves setting aside a period of time to deliberately focus your mind on a mental image of someone (or some creature) who is suffering, perhaps suffering in the same way that you are. Then you begin to pay attention to your breath. With each in-breath, you take in the pain of the sufferer, and with each out-breath, you let it carry only goodness and joy to the suffering person. Sometimes I find it easier to spend a portion of my *tonglen* time concentrating on taking on the pain of the sufferer with both in- and out-breaths, and another period of time sending out good things to that person. I also find it helpful to remind myself that pain shared is half the pain and joy shared is twice the joy. You will need to find what works best for you, but *how* you specifically do *tonglen* is not as important as *doing* it.

In my seminars on brokenness, I usually tell people about my use of *maitri* to help me work with the pain of my mother's departure from my life. Then, I describe how I set aside additional time some days to practice *tonglen* for other adults just like me, people who have the mistaken notion that something they did as a child drove a beloved parent away. During my *tonglen*, I spend a few minutes consciously trying to unburden others of their anguish by taking it on myself. Then I think of a joy in my life and spend several minutes sending it on to them. I usually come away from my *tonglen* meditation feeling more peaceful and more hopeful. And that takes me back to my practice of *maitri* and feeling more friendly toward myself.

When I share this experience, often someone gets a skeptical look and says something like this: "That's very sweet, but isn't that just wishful thinking? What possible difference can that *really* make to others who suffer? And why would I want to take on more pain? Isn't my own pain enough?"

I usually respond to this skepticism by *agreeing*! In fact, I will be the first to acknowledge that the *tonglen* meditation process may not have any direct impact on those who are suffering. I simply don't know. What I do know is that *tonglen* impacts me.

Since I have begun practicing *tonglen*, when I meet suffering people or hear the stories of those whose lives have been shattered, I find myself acting toward them in a way that is more compassionate, more loving. When I am in situations of strife or conflict, I find myself doing things that short-circuit the "I'm hurt, so I will strike back" reflex that I once so often employed. Instead, I find myself unconsciously looking for what pain may lie behind people's actions. I ask them what's going on, how they are feeling. More often than not, I find that people who hurt me are acting out of the same pain that causes *me* to say and do things that cause other people pain. My compassion for my own pain grows out of my compassion for theirs.

A few months after my accident in New Mexico, I began receiving physical therapy for the swelling and stiffness resulting from my RSD. During one of my first sessions, I noticed another patient who was also receiving therapy on one of her hands. Every time I saw Barbara (as I will refer to her), she seemed to be really struggling. She winced every time the therapist touched her hand, and she resisted taking part in most of the therapies suggested to her.

So, once I had come to grips with the fact that my hand might never again be whole, I decided to do *tonglen* for Barbara. I set my timer and spent ten minutes picturing and trying to feel the pain in Barbara's hand. As I meditated, I got a clear picture of her right hand frozen in a tightly clenched fist. (In an interesting contrast, my own injured left hand started out by being frozen in an *open* position.) As I continued to meditate on Barbara and her hand, I began to picture her sitting at the table where she did her therapy. I became aware that her body was hunched over and gathered in, mirroring the clenched position of her hand. She seemed to nestle her hand as though it were a tiny baby, and her face showed great sadness, fear, and depression. In subsequent periods of *tonglen* meditation, I alternated periods when I took on Barbara's pain and depression with periods when I sent her feelings of happiness.

Though I haven't seen Barbara in a while, and I have no idea whether my *tonglen* is making any difference in her life, I do know that my *tonglen* practice for her has made an important qualitative difference in my own life. The palpable feeling of connection with Barbara has eased my loneliness. The compassion I now feel for Barbara and her hand increases my compassion for myself during those times when I struggle with persistent discomfort. *Tonglen* practice also makes it easier for me to adopt an attitude of lovingkindness toward this particular manifestation of my brokenness. In addition, my practice of *tonglen* for one person has given me the strength to modify my practice further and expand it to include the suffering of all those who suffer in the way that Barbara does. I'm not sure what the final outcome will be, but I do know that this connection with an entire community of people like me has helped reduce my own physical and emotional pain dramatically as I continue on my journey toward mending.

GIVING *TONGLEN* A TRY

In her book *When Things Fall Apart*, Pema Chödrön outlines a very helpful step-by-step approach to practicing *tonglen*, which I have adapted for our context of working with brokenness. I suggest that you begin with two preliminary steps.

- First, spend an initial meditation session trying to feel and (where applicable) picture the brokenness of the person (or group) who is suffering and with whom you want to make a connection, especially between their pain and your own pain.

- Second, once you have a good sense of this brokenness, use another meditation session to ask the spirit of that person (or group) for permission to do *tonglen*. After meditating in this way, if you don't feel that you have permission to proceed, turn your attention to a different person or group and repeat the process. You may need to do this more than once. Continue until you feel you have permission. It is crucial to approach this process with a sense of respect and compassion for the person or persons you envision. Once you can feel and perhaps visualize the brokenness, and once you feel that you have permission to proceed, continue with the following steps to begin your own practice of *tonglen*.

Start out, as you did for *maitri*, with the following steps:

- Set a specific length of time for your *tonglen*. I use twenty minutes, but you may find a different length of time works better for you. And, depending on the person or people you choose to focus on for your *tonglen*, the time may vary as well.
- Choose a quiet place for your meditation.
- Sit on a mat or in a straight-back chair, whichever is the most comfortable for you.
- Remember to sit up straight, not in a slouch. If you're sitting on a chair, place your feet flat on the floor a comfortable shoulder-width apart.
- Fold your hands in your lap or place them palms down on your thighs.
- If possible, sit facing a blank wall so you won't be distracted by the "view."
- You can either close your eyes or keep them half open and unfocused (or focus on an object or point).
- Consciously relax all the parts of your body, beginning with your feet, moving on to your calves, and continuing on until you have relaxed your face and head.
- Once you have relaxed, begin getting in touch with your feelings, especially your pain (physical or emotional).
- Note where you feel your pain and how strong it is.

At this point in the meditation, the process begins to take a different direction than *maitri*:

- Picture someone (or a group of people, or a creature) who is suffering the same way you are.
- Begin breathing in and out at a slow, measured pace.

- On your in-breath, consciously take on the suffering and pain endured by the person(s) you are picturing.
- Try to feel that pain in the same way you do your own in the *maitri* practice, with deep compassion.
- On your out-breath, send your person(s) health, joy, and comfort.
- Repeat the in-breath/out-breath process for as long as you meditate.

After practicing *tonglen* for a while, you may begin to get a general sense of the relief your person(s) might be feeling now that their pain has been taken on by someone else. Also note how good it might feel for your person(s) to receive the health, joy, and comfort you have sent.

Using Sabbath, *Maitri*, and *Tonglen* Together

"In order to feel compassion for other people, we have to feel compassion for ourselves." That is the essence of Pema Chödrön's teaching about *maitri* and *tonglen*. If you are suffering from a sense of brokenness, I would also encourage you to consider the reverse of this statement: "In order to feel compassion for myself, I need to feel compassion for others." When you begin to have compassion for others, you may discover not only that your attitude toward other people changes but also that your attitude toward your own brokenness changes. As you begin to share your compassion, your compassion for yourself may expand as well.

That's what happens for me, through *tonglen*. Being more compassionate to others frequently results in my being a bit more compassionate to myself. Then I use that extra self-compassion in my *maitri* practice. And as I become more compassionate toward myself, I find it easier to sit quietly and practice a Sabbath time of "do nothing"—even when "the embarrassment of being me" rears its ugly head. The three meditation techniques of *maitri*, *tonglen*, and Sabbath are a powerful combination to help you gain a deeper and more compassionate awareness of your brokenness, and the brokenness of others, and prepare you for further steps on your road to mending.

4

LECTIO DIVINA

Understanding Your Brokenness

THE POWER OF STORY

I recently attended a lecture delivered by the eloquent Rabbi Lawrence Kushner, author of *Invisible Lines of Connection: Sacred Stories of the Ordinary* (Jewish Lights) among other books, and he reminded us that we can't really understand incidents in our past without connecting them to events in our present lives. He also pointed out the converse, that our present stories don't make sense unless we connect them to their seeds in our past, and in the context of our future.

For those of us who have a sense of brokenness, this suggests an important step in our mending: By studying our personal stories and reexamining our formative years when our feelings of brokenness began, we can begin to transform our experience of suffering. With the perspective of time and maturity, we can better understand the seminal incidents that shaped our brokenness.

In many ways, our stories define who we are. What we believe about ourselves—as well as what we reject—forms an essential part of our identity. Our stories have power over us. The lasting "truth" of our stories is what we hold on to, far beyond what actually happened. When we replay our personal stories in our minds, after a period of time it is not so much the facts of the events that carry the greatest significance, but the impact of those events on our sense of self, our relationships, and the world around us. These stories retain their power precisely because they are more than just facts; we imbue our stories with meaning.

If we relive moments of happiness and triumph, we may see ourselves as capable or talented, and feel energized or inspired to move forward. Remembering a long-ago sports win, for example, may translate the idea that "We won" into "I'm a winner." But for those of us who have a sense of brokenness, we are more often likely to reexperience darker times, to convert "We lost" into "I'm a loser." Indeed, some of our darker stories can haunt us, and sometimes we just can't help but replay them. It's a little like rubbing your tongue over a sore tooth. Even though it brings up the pain afresh every time, somehow you can't stop yourself from doing it.

While our personal stories can inform, they can also fossilize over time, and we can get into a rut with them. They can become calcified and eventually take on a form where the details remain essentially the same. If we rehearse the same old details, this gives rise to the same old feelings. That's why I want to introduce you to the ancient and revered technique of *Lectio Divina*, a Latin term meaning "sacred reading," or "divine reading." It was originally developed by medieval monks who wanted to gain maximum insight from their reading of scripture.

The techniques of *Lectio Divina* can be a very helpful way to explore your personal story with a kind of careful devotion, so you can get out of old ruts and move into a new understanding of the birth of your brokenness. The tool of *Lectio Divina* is a way to see your life story as holy—because it *is* holy—and to engage with your life story in a new way.

TRADITIONAL *LECTIO DIVINA*

Perhaps the best way to get to the heart of what *Lectio Divina* really is about is to begin with an explanation of how I first heard about *Lectio Divina* and connected it to my spiritual life.

In the mid-nineties I was living in Birmingham, Alabama, after completing work on a graduate degree. I was working in a dead-end job, my marriage was crumbling, and I was well on my way to becoming an alcoholic. In my desperation, I reached out for anything and everything that I thought might help me. I found a therapist, started going to twelve-step meetings, and began to explore the depths of my religious experience as a Roman Catholic.

Part of that religious journey led me to search for a spiritual director, a well-trained religious leader who could, in ways similar to a therapist, guide me through the questions and challenges I was facing. I made a connection with an eighty-year-old spiritual director named Sister Josepha McNutt, who began my spiritual direction with an inventory of my spiritual life. When she asked me to describe any spiritual practices I engaged in that brought fulfillment to my life, I had to admit that I didn't really have any—except, perhaps, reading stories from the Bible. They felt real for me. When I read them, I felt present in the stories; I could see, hear, smell, and practically taste what was going on in them. Josepha told me that this was actually a variation of an ancient Christian practice called *Lectio Divina*, and she proceeded to introduce me to the technique.

She explained that *Lectio Divina* can be traced to a twelfth-century Carthusian monastic named Guigo II, who described it in a book called *The Ladder of Monks*. The Ladder, according to Guigo II, had four steps, or rungs, that would lead us into the presence of God: reading, meditation, prayer, and contemplation.

To get a grasp of how *Lectio Divina* works, I'm going to walk you through an example of using *Lectio Divina* with a story from the Christian New Testament. Take a moment now to read through the story quickly, just to learn its details. Then, I'll show you how the practice of *Lectio Divina* can open up for you a deeper understanding.

From there [Jesus] set out and went away to the region
of Tyre. He entered a house and did not want anyone
to know he was there. Yet he could not escape notice,
but a woman whose little daughter had an unclean
spirit immediately heard about him, and she came and
bowed down at his feet. Now the woman was a
Gentile, of Syrophoenician origin. She begged him to
cast the demon out of her daughter. He said to her, "Let
the children be fed first, for it is not fair to take the children's food and throw it to the dogs." But she answered
him, "Sir, even the dogs under the table eat the children's crumbs." Then he said to her, "For saying that,
you may go—the demon has left your daughter." So she
went home, found the child lying on the bed, and the
demon gone. —MARK 7:24–30

This is the "bare bones" of the story. With the four steps of
Lectio Divina—reading, meditation, prayer, contemplation—it's
possible to go much deeper into the story and understand it at
different levels. The process itself is deliberate, unhurried, and
expansive, so it calls for slowing down to immerse yourself in
the experience.

Step 1: Reading

A monk in Guigo II's time would have started the *Lectio Divina*
process by reading the passage many times, going over it daily,
sometimes for weeks, occasionally for months, even on the rare
occasion for a year or longer, in order to gain maximum familiar-
ity with the text. Guigo II expected the reader to approach the
text with what he called "the soul's whole attention," paying close
attention to every word and phrase, how the words and phrases
were ordered, the literal and figurative meanings of every word,
and even what remained unspoken in the text.

One way to focus your "whole attention" on the text is to jot
down the key words and phrases that catch your attention as you

read the story. What seems interesting? Odd? Troubling? For example, among the key words I noted during my reading were "Gentile," "begged," "dogs," and "crumbs." The phrases "Let the children be fed first," "It is not fair," and "For saying that, you may go" also caught my eye.

The second phase of the reading step is to begin closely investigating every nuance of these words and phrases. This might involve looking up words in dictionaries and looking for other places in scripture where the same words are used. It also might mean considering the words and phrases from many different perspectives. For example, I wondered what it meant that the woman was a Gentile, that she was an outsider. Why was she compared to a dog? What was the significance of Jesus giving her what she wanted "for saying that"? If she hadn't said what she did, would she have been turned away? The ultimate goal of the reading step, over time, is to explore every nuance of every word and phrase that strikes you. But it is important not to try to do too much in any given *Lectio Divina* session. Remember, monks sometimes spent weeks and months on a single passage.

Regardless of the progress you might make in any given session of *Lectio Divina*, the reading step is always followed by the other three steps of *Lectio Divina*. Though each of the four steps of *Lectio Divina* represents a distinct phase, they are intended to be practiced together, in order, during every *Lectio Divina* session. If you isolate the steps—doing one each day, for example—you will lose the powerful combined effect of the *Lectio Divina* process.

Step 2: Meditation

The second step in the *Lectio Divina* process is meditation, but the term carries a different meaning than the typical idea of sitting in silence for extended periods of time to clear the mind and focus on something. As Guigo II used the word in the twelfth century, meditation meant to ponder something, to chew and break up a text so that the mind could discover the meaning of the text underneath the obvious or "plain" meaning of the words and phrases. This kind of meditation is a process of finding the deeper significance of the text.

Another way to think of it is to picture the reading step as *deconstructing* the text and the meditation step as *putting it all back together again* in a way that connects the story with your life. One way to do this is to let your list of key words and phrases guide you into a deeper understanding of the text and what meaning it might have for you. For example, one of the phrases that struck me immediately in the reading step was Jesus's words to the woman, "For saying that, you may go." Why did Jesus say, "For saying that"? Was he rewarding her persistence? Did he admire her impertinence? The insistence of this woman resonated deeply with me. I, too, have felt the need to ask for—even demand, when I don't receive an answer—help not only in my mending but also for God's intervention to help friends and loved ones. This is true even though I have often felt like an outsider (just as the woman in the story was a Gentile) and somehow unworthy of God's attention.

This kind of deep pondering takes time, and it is important to remember that the monks almost certainly would not have completed their meditation in a single sitting, or even in a few. However, even if you want to continue your meditation another time, remember, it is important to conclude your meditation period with the third and fourth *Lectio Divina* steps of prayer and contemplation.

Step 3: Prayer

The third step in the *Lectio Divina* process, prayer, was for Guigo II "the heart's devoted attending to God, so that evil may be removed and good may be obtained." Every time the monk entered a time of prayer following a *Lectio Divina* meditation session, he would gather in his mind all that he had learned and talk to God about it in a very personal way. He would ask for God's help to get the most out of the text.

It might help you to think of prayer as inviting wisdom directly into the *Lectio Divina* process as a partner to help you wrestle with the questions that arose during your meditation. The prayer step might take the form of actually praying or talking to God or your Higher Power, or if you are not comfortable with that, perhaps in the form of intentional journaling about your thoughts and feelings.

I often see myself as an outsider because of my broken-ness, so one of the key questions that arose for me after medi-tating on the reading was, "How far am I willing to go in pounding on heaven's door to demand God's intervention on my behalf?" (No wonder the word "beg" and the phrase "for saying that" leapt out at me during the reading.) I realized that I was not using all of the forms of prayer available to me to lay siege to heaven and trust that my prayers would be answered in some way. I began to direct my prayer to asking for help— something that is not easy for me to do.

Step 4: Contemplation

When the monk was finished talking to God, he would do some-thing that few of us do: he would sit still and listen. Guigo II's final step, contemplation, was simply to wait quietly in the presence of the Holy, being open and listening attentively and devotedly, for an answer to the prayers of the third step. Whereas prayer involves mental activity and effort, sitting in contemplation is an opportunity to wait and listen for whatever words or thoughts come to mind, to be aware of whatever images or sensations or feelings you experience. It is a time that can open you to the pos-sibility that, in the coming hours or days, you might experience a sense of response in the form of dreams, synchronicities, or other events that might occur in your life.

BRINGING *LECTIO DIVINA* TO BROKENNESS

The steps of *Lectio Divina* are pretty straightforward, but they call for a devotion of spirit and energy that asks us to bring our entire mind, body, and soul to the study of sacred stories—especially our own. I use the word "sacred" intentionally to describe our life stories because they encompass our most formative moments. Our lived experiences form the foundations of our core values and our fundamental view of ourselves and the world, and our stories deserve our greatest respect. As we learn to interpret and understand our stories in new ways, they can provide clues or insight that can aid in our mending process.

Most of us have a "stable" of stories, often from our childhood, that our minds return to again and again. Knowing which stories will be most fruitful to use with *Lectio Divina* isn't always easy, but sometimes a story will choose you. A story may keep coming up in your memory when you least expect it. It may be a story that seems to haunt you. It may well be a story that enacts the central issues and conflicts in your emotional life, the story that you, in some way, relive over and over in your relationships and in your work to overcome your sense of brokenness.

There is one such story from my life that I call "The Basement." Just why I have replayed this story for years is something of a mystery to me, but perhaps there is something in me that believes that if I could only do or say the right thing in my reenactments of the story, I would somehow be healed of the sense of brokenness that haunts me. Perhaps this is something like the experience of the main character in the film *Groundhog Day.* In essence, he was forced to relive the same day over and over (with some variations) until he "got it right." Unfortunately, he had no idea what it was that he had to do to "get it right." So, he pressed on, trying one change after another in the hope that something he did would liberate him from the strange loop in which he was trapped.

This loop feels familiar. For many years I struggled to gain a sense of the deep meaning of the events that occurred one very cold night in a basement when I was eight, but I failed. The only thing reliving the story ever did was to reinforce the pain and confusion that the event caused. But when I discovered the spiritual tool of *Lectio Divina,* I was able to use the process to connect my adult sense of brokenness with this critical event of my childhood, and to begin to find some mending.

As I will suggest you do with your own story, I began by writing my story down. This is an important part of the process; the very act of *writing* our stories is crucial because it is a way of capturing details, and it provides a base to refer back to as we move through the process. Here is my story as I wrote it:

The Basement

It was late in the winter of 1958–59. I had just turned eight. I was in bed in my Aunt Helen's unheated basement in a suburb about thirty miles south of Chicago. The temperature outside was well below freezing; inside the basement, it wasn't much warmer.

I had been sleeping in that basement since the previous summer, when my mother, Mary Ellen, and I had suffered the humiliation of being evicted from our low-income apartment by the sheriff. He had, literally, put our furniture out on the curb. I didn't know if we had been evicted because my mother couldn't pay the rent (even though my dad paid child support) or because of my mother's business interest in romance with men.

Aunt Helen was my mother's sister. Even though Helen had a husband, three young children, and a dog to take care of, she gave in to her sister Mary Ellen's tearful pleas for shelter and took the two of us in. The deal was that I would spend my waking hours with Aunt Helen's family, but at night I would sleep in the basement. I would be alone because my mother worked at night and slept during the day.

My suitemate at night was the family German shepherd who not only slept in the basement but also used its bare concrete floor as his bathroom.

I slept in the bed that my mother and Aunt Helen had salvaged from the curb after the eviction. The bed faced the bare pine-plank stairs that led up to the family kitchen. When darkness came, my mother tucked me in, the door to the kitchen was closed and locked, and I was left alone in the dark until morning.

As autumn changed to winter and the basement grew colder at night, I began to complain about the chill. More blankets and covers were added. I said that I was still cold. The answer to this complaint was a hot-water bottle that was placed at my feet under the many layers of covers. I remember that, at first, the bottle was so hot it burned my feet. My mother wrapped it in a towel, and I was encouraged to wear my socks to bed.

Then, one particularly icy night in February right after my eighth birthday, something in me snapped. Suddenly I felt that I couldn't spend another night alone in the dark. When my mother tucked me in, I begged her not to leave. I cried. I wailed. I pleaded. I threw a fit. I was inconsolable. Finally, my mother gave in and lay down beside me on the bed.

She waited until I dozed off and then stole up the stairs and off to her job.

At some moment in the night, I awakened and realized that I was once again alone in the dark and cold. For the first time in my life, I felt rage. That's a harsh word to use for the emotions of an eight-year-old, but I still remember that hot feeling. I had trusted my mother, and she had lied to me; I hated her and would never trust her again.

I didn't sleep again that night. Two months later my mother left my life, and I didn't see her again until I buried her nearly twenty years later.

ॐ

Once I had written my story, I was ready to begin the *Lectio Divina* process. I'll briefly summarize how my process evolved, and what I learned from it, to give you a few ideas about how you might be able to use *Lectio Divina* with your own story.

Step 1: Reading

I began by treating my story as if it had been written by someone else and I was simply analyzing it.

The first time I read through the story, I simply paid attention to what caught my attention. Because the child was locked in at night, I was struck by the parallels between the basement and a prison. A second reading drew my attention to the writer's use of the word "humiliation," and the literal and metaphorical humiliations the child suffered: being evicted, being forced to live in an unheated basement with dog excrement, knowing at age eight that his mother was a prostitute. The third reading drew my attention to the fact that the writer used gentle metaphors to speak of some of the horrible details: The mother wasn't referred to as a prostitute; she had a "business interest in romance with men." The dog was spoken of as a "suitemate."

Step 2: Meditation

As I meditated on these impressions, I probed for the meaning of the story underneath the obvious words and phrases. I came away with a sense of the child I was in this story: someone who had suffered so much shame that he couldn't admit the pain to himself and, instead, let it spill over into rage at his mother for putting him into a series of emotionally devastating and physically harmful situations. I saw how my effort to keep my mother at my side that night, as I threw a tantrum, might have been a symbolic way of responding to the looming prospect of my mother's permanent departure from my life.

Step 3: Prayer

During the time I spent in prayer after reading and meditating, I found myself, at first, asking to be able to forget this story. But as I prayed, I shifted to asking God to help me transform the way I looked at it so I could use its deeper meaning to regain a sense of wholeness within my brokenness.

Step 4: Contemplation

After sitting in contemplation, I had the sense that I had not completed my work with this story and needed to stay with it. I was aware only that the meaning for me lay hidden in the answer to the question, "Why did the events of that night affect me so profoundly?"

In the days and weeks that followed, each time I replayed the story, I found myself returning to this question. I came to understand that the answer lay in a truth that I didn't want to face: that, as a child, I *was* helpless. This was difficult to confront because my nature is such that I want to control situations. Perhaps replaying this story over and over again in my mind was my way of trying to find a way to control it, maybe even change it in some way. But engaging the story through the process of *Lectio Divina* helped me see that, as a child of eight, I was, in fact, helpless. Even more critically, I realized that as long as I continued to fight that reality, I would remain locked in that cold, dark basement. I would remain helpless. Paradoxically, seeing and accepting that I was helpless actually enabled me to let go of the struggle. Through *Lectio Divina*, I am now no longer helpless over this story.

Applying the process of *Lectio Divina* to my story helped me break out of the rut that this story had reinforced in my life. It wasn't so much a matter of "getting over" this story once and for all, but rather giving me a fresh perspective on it, allowing me to transform it from a source of pain to a source of insight, understanding, and in a small way, mending. The tools of *Lectio Divina* helped me face some difficult truths about myself. Above all, it gave me choices for ways to engage the story on my own terms—not as the fossilized, painful memory it had become.

BRINGING *LECTIO DIVINA* TO YOUR STORY

Perhaps as you've been reading this, you've been thinking, "*Lectio Divina* sounds like a lot of work!" You're right; it is. The process of applying *Lectio Divina* to your personal story will take time and effort—but that is its very strength, for the detailed work can help you discover new perspectives. I urge you to give it a try to see what you might discover.

Start by making a written list of the childhood or other events around which you have constructed your life story. Even though you may be tempted to list these events mentally, it is important to record them with pen and paper, or on your computer, or in whatever way is most comfortable for you. I suggest that you make two lists, one of some positive events and the other of the darker, negative events; *Lectio Divina* works equally well with both.

To illustrate what I mean, here's a partial list of some events in my life that serve as core elements to my story:

Positive

- When I was eight years old, my father rescued me when my mother disappeared from my life.
- Through my stepfamily I began to attend church.
- I set the record as the fourth worst batter in the history of Little League baseball, but through it learned to overcome fears that paralyzed me.
- When I was ten years old, I had my first spiritual experience at summer camp.
- In the fifth grade I pulled myself up from the "average" to the "advanced" reading group in just one week.
- I decided when I was twelve that I wanted to be a minister when I grew up because that would allow me to live like Jesus.
- My first poem was published when I was sixteen.

Negative

- When I was five years old, I was taken away from my mother and sent to live with an aunt and uncle for a year.
- During first grade, my best friend died of leukemia.
- My mother and I were evicted from our low-income apartment and had our furniture put out on the curb. She and I spent the next year sleeping in my aunt's unheated basement.

- Just after I moved in with my father and his new wife, I almost died from the measles when my fever reached 106°F.
- I was so alienated from my family that I emotionally disengaged from life and immersed myself in a world of books, movies, and TV programs.
- Over a seven-year period, I was physically, emotionally, and (later) sexually abused by a family member.
- Because of the despair I felt about my family situation, I started smoking when I was twelve.
- I witnessed the death of my older stepbrother, Jimmy, who shot himself in the heart.
- When I was fifteen, I made a halfhearted attempt at suicide.

Obviously, your list of events will be different from mine. As you write down the positive and negative events in your life that replay in your mind, try to do it without judgment. These are events that have happened, and you are simply noting the fact of their occurrence.

Now that you have an idea of what the *Lectio Divina* process entails, allow yourself some time to consider which event on your list seems like one that *Lectio Divina* might best help you engage. Which of these events speaks to you the most about your brokenness now?

When you have chosen one, sit down with a pen and paper, or at your computer, and write your story of this event in as much detail as you can muster. This step of writing out your story is crucial. Even if you have mentally rehearsed the story countless times, the very details that come out while writing it are often the most revealing—and the most helpful. Consider these things as you write your story:

- Once you start, don't stop. Complete the story in a single sitting, no matter how long it takes.
- Don't edit yourself. Remember, no one will read this story but you, and you can destroy it or delete it later if you want.

Rough edges, strange words, misspellings—these are all important details that can yield surprising insights later. Trying to craft a smooth story, as if you wanted to publish it, will likely gloss over or ignore some excellent (and perhaps painful) details. The result will be a less effective *Lectio Divina* practice.

- Make sure that you tell the event as an action story that has a setting, a character, and action. Put yourself in the story, using the "I" pronoun. Note the setting, the date or year, the names and roles of people who were involved in the event, how you felt, and anything else you can remember. No detail is too small or insignificant. Put the story into motion. Give it historical context.
- Don't overly concern yourself with the question, "Did it really happen that way?" The facts are important, but if your imagination has created a detail that didn't actually happen, chances are good that the detail you remember reveals a significance deeper than the facts seem to bear out. Trust your instincts.
- Pay attention to details that seem insignificant. If they are present in your memory, they have been preserved by your mind for a reason!

When you are done, resist the urge to read back over your story immediately. Instead, put it away for a day or two.

When you are ready to begin your *Lectio Divina*, create a time and space where you won't feel hurried and won't be disturbed. Give this process the amount of time it deserves. Remember, you are dealing with "scripture," your own sacred story. I would suggest at least an hour, but tailor the time to meet your own spiritual needs.

Step 1: Reading

Read your written story slowly and reflectively, several times, so that the words sink in. Jot down the particular words and phrases that catch your attention. It's okay to have just a few entries, or a dozen or two, or more.

Step 2: Meditation

Consider the words you've jotted down. Why do you think these particular words called to you? How do you think they connect with your brokenness?

Step 3: Prayer

Take the questions, issues, joy, or anguish you experience in reliving this story to God, your Higher Power, or your inmost self.

Step 4: Contemplation

Let go of "thinking," and open your heart and mind to the thoughts, images, and feelings that come to you.

❦

As the monks of the twelfth century did, I suggest that you repeat the *Lectio Divina* process with your story several, if not many, times. Each time you work with your story, you may learn something new. You may also find that, over time, the deeper meaning of your story changes. There is a group of South American shamans who suggest telling your story *twenty-eight* times! In their practice, the story remains pretty much the same in meaning for the first twenty-seven times, but reverses the polarity of its meaning on the twenty-eighth telling. Your experience may not be so dramatic. Still, revisiting your story five or ten or twenty times may offer some powerful insights. You may also find it helpful to journal about your experience immediately following each session of *Lectio Divina*. This will give you a record of your thoughts and feelings that you can refer back to at a later time.

TAKING *LECTIO DIVINA* ONE STEP FURTHER

As powerful a tool as *Lectio Divina* is, you can take it to another dimension through a profoundly effective technique that I call "immersion experience." It is a way of immersing yourself in the story from different viewpoints, putting yourself into the shoes of each character and trying to experience his or her emotions. What thoughts and feelings would you have if you had been that person? By engaging the emotions of each character, you move beyond *thinking* about the story to *feeling* it as well. In turn, this opens up new ways of understanding why the story goes the way it does, and gives new opportunities to make choices about how you might feel about the story.

For example, when I reread "The Basement" story and put myself in my Aunt Helen's shoes, I realized that she must have been furious at having her life disrupted. She was forced to offer food and shelter to her sister and nephew against her will. I also felt her anguish at knowing that her nephew was sleeping each night in that unheated basement. And I felt her shame at having a sister who was a prostitute.

Putting myself in my father's shoes was a bigger challenge for me. He is briefly mentioned in the story but is most notable for his absence. I wondered if my father was aware of my sleeping arrangements. I felt my father's embarrassment at knowing that his ex-wife and the mother of his son had become a prostitute.

When it came to my mother, it was a challenge to understand what she must have been thinking and feeling. To the outside world, her life must have appeared to be in free fall. She probably felt like a pariah within her own family. She probably also felt that her son was a burden she could not carry. Understanding this possibility helped me begin to consider the possibility that my mother may have been suffering, too. This realization gave me a sense of compassion for her for the first time.

From my own perspective as a child, I felt as though I were being punished for something I hadn't done. I felt like an outsider in the family within which I dwelt. I wanted love and protection, but I felt fear—and immense rage. I saw that, as a child, I was truly helpless in that situation.

When I looked at this story from the perspective of an adult, I was left in a state of outrage at all of the adults in the story.

Whatever was going on in their own lives, each of these individuals was giving tacit approval to a situation that, in today's world, would be considered child abuse and endangerment. More important, I also realized that even though I was mostly helpless as an eight-year-old, I did speak up and try to do something to change my situation. Even though I failed to get what I wanted that night, my circumstances did, in fact, change shortly thereafter. As an adult, this was a powerful realization.

If you want to try this "immersion experience" with your own story, I recommend following it with a period of meditation, prayer, and contemplation, as with traditional *Lectio Divina*. It is important to keep every one of your senses open to the possibility of a contemplative communication from the Divine or from your heart.

In conclusion, there is one more suggestion I'd like to pass on to you: as you continue to read and work with your life stories, courageously ask yourself if all of the details of each story are true and accurate. I have learned much about this from the spiritual leader Byron Katie, who offers a method called "The Work" for testing the truth of our stories. She suggests that we simply ask ourselves, "Is it true? How can I absolutely know that this is true?" as a way to examine the reality of the situation.

If you find that one or more of your stories don't hold up to close examination, take some time to explore the implications of that insight. What does this new truth mean? If one or more of the details of your story has changed, how does that affect the meaning of the story at the time it took place? Of equal, if not more, importance is the question of how the change affects the meaning of the story for you today. Finally, if you encounter a change in perception, how does this affect your sense of brokenness?

THE IMPACT OF *LECTIO DIVINA*

We all create the stories of our lives in our minds. But like the famous folktale "The Blind Men and the Elephant," what we keep in mind is inevitably only part of the story, and the part we recall most vividly may not be helpful in addressing our brokenness. By revisiting and exploring the details of our life stories from a variety of perspectives, we may discover additional elements that allow us to see our brokenness in a different light. We can gain insight and increase compassion for ourselves.

As Rabbi Kushner advised, we can't really understand the present without understanding the meaning of our past. *Lectio Divina* gives us a chance to understand our past with the perspective we have gained over the years.

When you select key stories from the vast panorama of events in your life, it can help bring focus to *why* you are who you are. When you review the details of your formative years (both positive and negative), it can help you put together the jigsaw puzzle of scattered and seemingly unrelated details of your life story. Reviewing those details may awaken you to important details of and feelings about your current situation. Moreover, focusing on the key event or events in the development of your brokenness will help you see your brokenness more clearly.

When you spend time with your life stories, going over and over them, you may begin to recover significant events you had forgotten. Armed with additional details, you may begin to see your brokenness from a new perspective. When you apply the various types of *Lectio Divina* to your stories, you can begin to view your memoir with a sense of sacredness. There is great benefit in treating the events of your life as what they really are: sacred stories that deserve the care and attention, the reflection and exploration, that you would devote to the most revered text in your spiritual practice. Practicing the slow, deliberate steps of *Lectio Divina* with your life experiences can transform your stories from sources of pain to sources of understanding, and bring you closer to mending your brokenness.

5

PILGRIMAGE

Finding Meaning in Your Brokenness

WHY GO ON A PILGRIMAGE?

Have you ever revisited a place that had significant personal meaning for you? Perhaps you've made a trip back to the neighborhood where you grew up but long since left behind. Or maybe you've visited an important historical site to reflect on what happened to your ancestors there. Or perhaps your journey was more of a pilgrimage of the heart, looking through old memorabilia or letters that you found in a parent's closet or attic.

In essence, a pilgrimage is a journey to a site that has the potential to connect us with something important in our lives and bring meaning to our experience. It is not a vacation or a trip to "get away from it all," but rather a journey to honor, to witness, to understand. It is the journey of a seeker looking for a connection, an answer, an insight, a resolution.

In their book *The Modern Pilgrim: Multidisciplinary Explorations of Christian Pilgrimage,* psychologists Paul Post, Jos Pieper, and Marinus van Uden report on their investigation into why people make pilgrimages today. In their study of pilgrims who went to

Lourdes, they found three primary motivations: "deepening of faith," "beseeching help and cure," and "looking for peace and quietness."

For those of us who live with a sense of brokenness, I would add a fourth motivation for a pilgrimage: to find meaning in our brokenness. Much has been written about the need to find meaning in our lives, from concentration camp survivor Viktor Frankl's *Man's Search for Meaning*, in which he said, "To live is to suffer, to survive is to find meaning in the suffering," to Carl Jung's statement that "Meaning makes a great many things endurable—perhaps everything."

I think this gets at the core of why you might want to consider making a pilgrimage to the site of the origin of your brokenness. When you can revisit and reexamine those critically important places, persons, and events that have played a crucial role in the development of your sense of brokenness, you have a sacred opportunity to look at your life and see it more clearly, to understand what happened and how it has affected you, and to find the meaning of these experiences in your life today. You can begin to reprocess your story and understand why you feel broken; you can begin to repair the damage from what is missing from your life. You may be able to begin rewriting your life story, creating a new narrative that gives your story a different and healthier meaning. Ultimately, your journey can help you find personal meaning in your suffering.

The locations of disasters and joys in your formative years are truly holy sites, and they are worthy of pilgrimage. The pilgrimage is not only a physical journey to a significant place from your past but also an inner spiritual journey. If you embark on this journey with your whole mind, heart, and soul, you can go deeper in your exploration of who you really are. To put it in the simplest terms, you can connect deeply with what formed your sense of brokenness so you can recover your complete self.

"If broken you will be sent home immediately." I saw those words on a sign recently. At first they gave me a chuckle, and then they gave me pause to think.

I was with friends gathered for a retreat in the community center at a Methodist church in Birmingham, Alabama, and the sign was on the wall in the room where we met, warning people not to bring alcohol or guns into the space. Its words captured my attention; its twisted, ungrammatical message about brokenness touched on something very important to me. Taking this sign literally offered a deeper insight about brokenness and about pilgrimage. It suggested to me that, once we have used *Lectio Divina* and other tools to explore and understand our brokenness, we should return home immediately—not necessarily "home" in a literal sense, but to the place where our brokenness began.

That trip probably won't be easy. By definition, pilgrimages are trips that offer challenges and difficulties to those who undertake them. I'll be honest and say that the tool offered in this chapter may be painful to use, but it might also offer you the greatest opportunity for mending if you undertake your pilgrimage with mindfulness.

THE POWER OF *HAJJ*

The idea of pilgrimage can be traced far back in historical and religious writings, from the biblical story of Abraham to the site of Buddha's enlightenment, and is present in almost all of the world's religions. Jews visit Jerusalem, Muslims travel to Mecca, Buddhists journey to Tibet, Hindus go to Varanasi, Christians make pilgrimages to the Holy Land or to Rome.

Pilgrimages have been undertaken by humans from the moment when our ancestors visited and revisited the sites of great hunting successes or the locations of battlefield victories. The ancient practice of pilgrimage is as popular today as it ever was, and destinations for modern pilgrims vary from Stonehenge, to the caves at Lascaux (with their beautiful prehistoric paintings), to the verdant jungles of the Amazon, and even to Graceland, Elvis's home in Memphis, Tennessee. Many of these places have historical significance, but sometimes their deeper meaning is derived from the reverence with which these sites are held by the pilgrims who come.

Over the years I have made many pilgrimages, visiting the homes of my favorite writers, the town that was home to St. Francis, and, yes, even Graceland. But for me, the most powerful model for a life-changing journey is the once-in-a-lifetime *hajj*, the mandatory pilgrimage that is one of the Five Pillars of Islam. *Hajj* means literally "to set out for a place," and for practicing Muslims, it means a pilgrimage to the spiritually important city of Mecca, a journey all able-bodied Muslims who can afford it are obliged to make. Here stands the Ka'ba, the central focus of the *hajj*, which Muslims believe to be the location of the Sacrifice of Abraham, an *axis mundi*, a virtual navel that connects heaven and earth.

I find the idea of a *hajj* compelling. For Muslim pilgrims, it is a journey to what they recognize as a key site in the spiritual history of humankind. But it is also, as Islamic professor Shahul Hameed puts it, "an exteriorization of an inner journey towards truth, or an adventure of spiritual discovery." For those of us who experience brokenness, making such a journey to the holiest sites of our personal history might well be one of the pillars of our own spiritual growth. Even though the trip we take may be to a site that has particular meaning only for us, it represents a sacred journey nonetheless.

Pilgrimages require us to leave the familiar to find something spiritually satisfying, something deeper than we currently know. We might come because we are in crisis, or we might come to find the truth of what happened to us in that place. But most of all, we come to seek mending, an inner peace, and empowerment over what keeps us feeling broken.

Phil Cousineau, author of *The Art of Pilgrimage: The Seeker's Guide to Making Travel Sacred*, points out that "pilgrims undertake arduous journeys because they believe that there is something vital missing in their lives. They sense that vitality itself may be lurking on the road or at the heart of a distant sanctuary." And he poignantly adds, "The ritual act of pilgrimage attempts to fill that emptiness."

A pilgrimage is not something to enter into casually. While a pilgrimage to a key place where your story developed can bring new meaning to your life, it can also be painful. Yet, paradoxically, the difficulty of such a journey can be essential to its meaning, and to your mending. The keys are preparation in advance and contemplation after its completion.

A FAILED *HAJJ*

In *The Art of Pilgrimage: The Seeker's Guide to Making Travel Sacred*, Cousineau carefully advises, "With a deepening of focus, keen preparation, attention to the path below our feet, and respect for the destination at hand, it is possible to transform even the most ordinary trip into a sacred journey, a pilgrimage." But unfortunately, the opposite is just as true: even the pilgrimage that holds the promise of being profound can be made mundane and meaningless if it is not undertaken with "keen preparation" and spiritual intent. I know because I made such a journey that was disappointing in large part because of my lack of thoughtful preparation. I didn't spend much time reflecting on its meaning before, during, or after.

I set out to make what I thought would be a once-in-a-lifetime *hajj* to the most sacred places in my personal development, starting with my hometown. I chose to visit, in a single day, three different houses that were key contributors to the development of my brokenness, as well as a summer camp one hundred miles away that had served as a refuge for me.

My first stop was a small, shoebox-shaped brick duplex where I had lived with my mother from age three to six— except for nine months during which I was wrenched from my mother's custody "for my protection" and sent to live with her sister and brother-in-law a few miles away. I don't recall my mother being abusive, but her vocation as a prostitute put me in situations that were inappropriate for a little boy and caused her to be, at best, neglectful of my physical, emotional, and educational needs.

On the morning of my pilgrimage, I stood on the curb in exactly the same spot where my mother and I had stood with our possessions after a sheriff had evicted us some forty-six years earlier. I gazed at a duplex that had, over the years, been transformed from a dingy apartment building with plain walls, cold linoleum floors, and the acrid odor of the coal used to heat it, to what was now a pleasant set of garden apartments with bright colors and lace drapes in the windows. I stood there for only a few minutes. I couldn't tell if anyone was home, but even if they were, I didn't have the courage to go up and knock on the door and ask to see the interior of my first home. I felt no emotion except a powerful need to get away from there as fast as I could.

I then headed for the place where my mother and I had taken up residence on the day we were evicted, and where we lived for the next year—her sister's unfinished, unheated basement. This time, I did walk up and ring the doorbell, but no one answered.

After a few minutes of poking around, I left, driving to the third location, where I had gone to live at the end of the basement year, after my mother had abandoned custody of me and disappeared. My father, who had just remarried, had taken me in to live with him in his new house with his new wife and her two sons. But when I arrived at that house, I never moved from the curb. I couldn't bear the idea of standing in the room where my teenage stepbrother had shot himself and died before my eyes when I was twelve. I couldn't bring myself to enter the house where a family member had repeatedly molested me. After only a minute, I got in my car and drove away as fast as I could.

Then I drove one hundred miles to Camp Lakewood. As I walked alone around the campground, I was taken back to why this place, more than any other in my childhood, felt like home.

Here we had worked, played, swum, ate, read, studied, and sang in a way that was gentle, caring, and respectful of each other. And we did all of this in a way that connected us with the natural world. Sadly, this last stop on my pilgrimage lasted no more than half an hour.

Any one of the places I visited on that day could have been the destination for a pilgrimage. Any one of them could have been the subject of weeks of emotional preparation. Any one of them could have been a destination at which I stopped and stayed and pondered. What could have been a *hajj* for me wasn't because I failed to put anything into it. I put absolutely no time or effort into preparing for the journey, did nothing to mark my departure, spent virtually no time at each of the stops on my journey, did nothing to mark the completion of the journey, and spent a total of about five minutes reflecting on the entire enterprise.

The day before this failed *hajj*, I had visited Chicago's Art Institute to see an exhibit of the works of the French post-impressionist painter Georges Seurat. I was fascinated by the way he created his paintings by placing dots of color side by side on the canvas so that the real impact of the work can only be experienced properly when the viewer stands back from the canvas ten or fifteen feet. In retrospect, I can see that the idea of taking a step back to gain perspective could have served as the metaphor for my *hajj*. If I had taken the time to step back from my experience and reflect on each stop, I might have had a much more meaningful experience.

But I didn't. I failed to make any deep connection with the process I was undertaking. I wish I had learned more about what goes into making a pilgrimage meaningful before I made that faux pilgrimage. I wish I had read a book such as Phil Cousineau's remarkable *The Art of Pilgrimage: The Seeker's Guide to Making Travel Sacred.* So, before you consider making your own *hajj*, I want to offer a few thoughts that will help you make your pilgrimage a valuable experience.

STAGES OF A PILGRIMAGE

I'm grateful to Phil Cousineau for his descriptions of pilgrimage, and in particular, his understanding of how a pilgrimage unfolds in distinct stages. As I've reflected on my own experience, I see my pilgrimages encompassing five stages, with an element, reflection, that is integral to each stage:

> Stage 1: The Call
> Stage 2: The Preparation
> Stage 3: The Journey
> Stage 4: The Arrival
> Stage 5: The Return

Stage 1: The Call

Before you start out on a pilgrimage, an idea usually gets you thinking about making this particular journey, to this particular place. You may start having memories of an important event or place from your past, or you may hear from someone you haven't heard from in a long time and start to think about an emotional encounter, or you may find yourself in a situation where you are traveling on a business or family matter in the area of a place where you experienced a childhood trauma. The more you reflect on the idea, the more you feel compelled to go back to this key place where a piece of your life story developed.

For some people, the call is not so obvious. If no one place comes immediately to mind, you might start by making a list of the people, places, and events that were critically important in the development of your sense of brokenness. As you make note of the powerful experiences of your formative years, one experience in particular may call to you. You may feel a surge of emotions as you recall a particular event and realize that this would be an important place to revisit.

However your past calls to you, ultimately, you are the only one who can decide when it is time to make a sacred journey to come face to face with a piece of your life story.

Stage 2: The Preparation

Preparation may well be the most important step in your pilgrimage process. Without careful, thoughtful, and heartfelt preparation, even a trip to the holiest place on the planet can end up as empty as a tourist "drive-by." Successful preparation includes careful attention to the specific details of your travel plans (including how much time you will need to allow for careful reflection on your experience—certainly not the four-places-in-one-day trip that I planned!). In addition, your preparation needs to include time for visualizing the journey before it happens and perhaps journaling on a number of important questions, such as:

> Why am I going?
> What do I hope to gain from the experience?
> What challenges or problems am I walking away
>   from?
> What challenges and opportunities am I walking
>   toward?

It is also important to prepare yourself for the emotional impact your sacred journey may have on you. You may have "moved on" from your childhood trauma in many ways, but encountering the place where these events took place could bring up unexpected emotions. Or perhaps you are currently struggling with some intense feelings that are linked with the place you will visit. It is important to make your *hajj* when you have the support you need, and when you have the time to process the feelings and memories your trip might bring to the surface. This trip should not be a threat to your well-being, but rather a fruitful spiritual journey to help mend your brokenness. I recommend that you think about a simple ritual or ceremony that you might perform for yourself when you reach your destination. Not only will it be a tool to help you honor the sacred nature of the site you are visiting, but it will also be a way to help you cope with your feelings when you arrive.

Stage 3: The Journey

The journey itself demands constant mindfulness and a commitment to, as Ram Dass would say, "be here now." Such a journey begs you to be aware constantly of how and what you are feeling, and of the need for self-care—not just for the blisters you may develop on your feet, but also for the blisters that may pop up on your emotions and on your soul.

If you have prepared yourself well, you won't need to spend the time of the journey thinking about getting to your destination or fretting about what emotions you may feel when you arrive. You may instead use the time of travel in a relaxing way, seeking comfort, being particularly mindful of what you encounter along the way.

While it isn't exactly possible to reflect on a journey while you are in progress, adopting an attitude of mindfulness as you travel can arm you with a special form of reflection-like experience that enables you to tune your mind and senses to a level of maximum awareness of what is happening around you. This will also help you reflect more fully at a later time.

Stage 4: The Arrival

After all the preparation and travel, you finally arrive at your destination. You've made it! But this stage of coming to the crux of your journey can be a double-edged experience. You might have a sense of joy at having achieved a goal after overcoming obstacles. You might "meet your demons," so to speak, or you might make a new kind of peace with your past. Your *hajj* might be the powerful spiritual experience you were looking for—or not. Either way, you might be left with a kind of postpartum depression that the journey is over. You might be asking, "Is that all there is?" This is a point where performing a ritual or ceremony can be very helpful in coping with powerful emotions and thoughts.

Give the experience the time and attention it deserves. Don't rush through your arrival. Before or after your ritual, you may want to embrace silence. If you are traveling with a friend or partner, you might want to spend time talking about the ideas and feelings you are experiencing. Even if you are traveling by yourself, you might want to use both spoken words and silence. Let your heart be your guide.

Stage 5: The Return

No pilgrimage is complete until you return home and begin to process what you have experienced. When you return, you will need to look at what you have brought back with you, by way of both physical treasure and emotional baggage. In this fifth stage, the element of reflection is perhaps the most crucial. Everything I know about travel and about struggle tells me that no pilgrimage is complete until the pilgrim has undertaken a period of deep reflection: savoring the moments of joy; wincing at the painful times; thinking about the meaning of the people and places encountered; recounting the events witnessed or in which you participated. I strongly urge you to take time, such as a Sabbath experience, to reflect on the meaning and implications of the journey you have undertaken. Making meaning of what has happened in all five stages is the point at which you can begin processing how your journey relates to your brokenness.

A Successful *Hajj*

Three years after my failed *hajj* to three different homes and a summer camp, I was ready to try again. I knew that part of the problem with the first pilgrimage was that I had done nothing to prepare, and as I visited my sacred sites, I had paid little attention to what I was doing. My next personal *hajj* unfolded in a much more thoughtful fashion.

Stage 1: The Call

The call for this second pilgrimage began almost the moment my failed pilgrimage ended. I was left with a persistent feeling that I needed to retrace my steps homeward, but this time with a mindfulness that could help me use the experience to mend my sense of brokenness. In the fall of 2007, as I was beginning a new relationship and recovering from my disastrous accident, I felt the need to make a repeat *hajj* to the same places I had visited so unsuccessfully. This time I would approach the pilgrimage with the specific intention of seeking closure about my connection to these sites that had been so emotionally disastrous for me as a child, and that continued to be prominent in my struggle to mend my brokenness.

Stage 2: The Preparation

This time around, I prepared myself by asking some probing questions about why I had decided to move this pilgrimage from a notion to a reality.

Why was I going? What did I hope to gain?

I realized that I still felt a gnawing need to reconnect with the dark places of my youth, and I needed to find some way to begin the process of letting go of the pain.

What comforts and challenges was I walking away from in making this journey?

It is tempting, when embarking on a pilgrimage, to focus only on what lies ahead on the road and not pay adequate attention to what is being left behind to make the journey. In leaving Louisville where I lived, I was certainly going to leave behind some of my pain and anguish (especially about my struggle to recover from my injuries), but in all honesty I knew I was also going to leave behind the comfort of familiar places, friends, habits, and routines, comforts that sometimes helped me gloss over the real pain of my situation instead of focusing on how to mend.

What challenges and opportunities did I face?

Perhaps the biggest challenge was the perceived threat that I might experience emotional pain that would force me to re-endure the tortures of my childhood (something I *really* didn't want to do). But that same threat also held the possibility that if I did reconnect with these sites, I might be able to find a way to unplug from them, or at least find a way to ease the pain I associated with them.

As I prepared for the trip, I first set the date (the day after Thanksgiving) and talked a great deal with my partner, Fran, whom I had invited to make the pilgrimage with me. We planned the trip together and included time for some fun activities, such as meals at some of my favorite restaurants, an overnight stay, and shopping at a bookstore I love. We also spent a good deal of time discussing the events that had happened at the three locations I wanted to visit. This talking, with time for Fran to ask questions about what had happened during my childhood, gave me a chance to review the events, and it also provided her information she needed in order to be a thoughtful and supportive partner on this pilgrimage.

Fran suggested a key element in the preparation for the trip: the design of a brief ceremony to be used at each of the three sites, accompanied by the creation of a small piece of art to be left at each stop. She had found a pattern for a very simple folded paper (origami) house. I made one such house for each stop and attached to each house a symbol of something positive that I associated with each place. For the first stop, it was a photograph of me riding a tricycle when I was three years old. For the second, it was a photocopy of a cassette tape of the Christmas song "The Little Drummer Boy." I had heard that song for the first time during the Christmas of 1958, at age seven, when the song first came out, and I realized that I was the little boy in the song: he was somebody who had no gift to give; he was poor and had nothing, just like me, but his gift of his drumming was acceptable. For the third house, I made a photocopy of the cover of the first Bible I ever owned. My intent in making these small pieces of art was to use them as a way of exorcising the psychological demons that still haunted me from these painful childhood places. By leaving behind at each stop an artifact of something positive that had happened there, I could turn my focus from the suffering I had experienced there to the things I had encountered there that gave me the strength to endure and thrive.

Stage 3: The Journey

Fran and I left in an atmosphere of tension early on the morning after Thanksgiving. The night before we had struggled through a fairly serious argument about the time of our departure. Both of us were anxious. The morning was sunny but cold. The drive was almost three hundred miles and lasted about five hours. We filled the lengthy drive not with talk about the serious events awaiting us, but rather with casual conversation and music from a few CDs we had brought along. We kept things light, and the tension seemed to lift as we neared our destination in northern Indiana.

One of the unexpected gifts of the pilgrimage was the encounters we had with places from my childhood that held pleasant memories: the library that nurtured my love of reading; the school where the teachers helped me see my gifts as a student; the park where, as a Little League baseball player, I learned to overcome my fear of failure. Fran and I chatted about these places, and our conversation was good preparation for the difficult encounters that lay ahead of us.

Stage 4: The Arrival

For reasons related to logistics, we made the stops of my first pilgrimage in reverse chronological order. We stopped first at the location where, from the ages of eight to fifteen, I had been multiply abused by a family member and where I had witnessed the death by suicide of my older stepbrother. My intention had been to try to enter each house, but at this first stop in the early afternoon, we rang the doorbell and no one answered. We walked back to the curb and left the little origami house with the picture of my Bible on it as our gift to this holy place. We took a photo (as we did at each stop) of what we had left. We stood there in silence for only a few minutes, invoking a spirit of mending, but it was enough.

The last stop of the day was similar. Later in the afternoon we visited the apartment from which my mother and I had been evicted when I was seven. There we rang the doorbell and were met by the current resident, an elderly woman. I told her that I had lived in this place when I was a child and asked if we could come in and look around. She politely declined. When she stepped back into her apartment and closed the door, Fran and I moved back to the street and left the paper house with the picture of me on the tricycle, again spending a few moments in silence.

It was the middle stop that was most powerful and the most troubling. On that stop we visited the house where "The Basement" story took place. We didn't expect anyone to be home, but when we rang the doorbell a man answered. I explained to him that my mother and I had lived in that house for a year when I was a child. I asked if Fran and I could come in. To my great surprise, he welcomed us in and let us look around.

The house had been remodeled and expanded, but its core elements were still there, although in a slightly different configuration than I recalled (in my memory the kitchen was in the front of the house when, in fact, it was in the back). We strolled through the hallways and peaked into a room or two. Then I braced myself for disappointment and asked our host if we could go down into the basement. He surprised me by acceding to this request as well, but warned that it was now used for storage. We descended the stairs into the darkness. We couldn't find a light switch. The moment we reached the basement floor, I wanted to leave as fast as I could. I had read somewhere that evil is dark and hot, and that space felt both to me. We didn't stay long. When we left the house, we paused as we had at the other sites and left a folded paper house, this one bearing the image of the "Little Drummer Boy" cassette. The period of silence was shorter here, the departure more urgent.

Stage 5: The Return

We took our time returning home, spending the night in a motel, shopping at the bookstore, making a whimsical decision to visit some artist friends, dining in another restaurant I loved. We didn't talk about the stops, the ceremonies, the encounters. We gave ourselves the space we needed to decompress.

Time for reflection came slowly and not by invitation. In all honesty, I wasn't as prepared as I thought I was for the feelings that filled my heart in the weeks and months that followed the pilgrimage. A depression set in, but a wonderful counselor offered suggestions about ways to cope. I also learned a bit more patience and embraced the not-so-easy process of practicing what I preach by employing the spiritual tools we are exploring together in this book.

As I was able to spend time reflecting on what had happened during my personal *hajj*, I came to a point of closure about the locations in my hometown and what had happened to me in those places. Not total closure, but at least the beginning point of letting go. I no longer felt any need to revisit those places—or the feelings associated with them. Someday I may just happen to be in my hometown, but it won't be by choice. I no longer have any reason to go there.

I do know, by hard experience, that dark feelings about those places will crop up from time to time in the future. But I now understand more of the damage I experienced at each pilgrimage site, and I feel better prepared to deal with these feelings as they arise.

HAJJ ALTERNATIVES

Sometimes it is not possible to make a trip back to the place or places associated with your brokenness. The distance may be too great. You may not have the finances to afford the travel. The emotional cost of physically standing in those places may be too much. There are other options, other ways to make a personal *hajj*.

A virtual pilgrimage. One option would be to take a "virtual" pilgrimage in which you imagine and write in great detail what such a journey would be like. The techniques of creative visualization can help you take a virtual pilgrimage by letting your imagination carry you back to your destination. In the same way that the immersion experience technique can help you go deeper into being in a story with *Lectio Divina* (see page 53), you can invoke all of your senses in imagining your *hajj* in as much detail as you like. Find a comfortable place, close your eyes, and imagine what you might see. What does the air feel like at your destination? Is it cold? Warm? Hot? Is there a wind or rain or snow? Do you feel pain? What emotions are you experiencing? Fear? Anger? Sadness? Happiness? Are you aware of aromas or odors? Does the experience leave any taste in your mouth? Bitter, sweet, salty? What sounds do you hear? Birds singing? Traffic whizzing by? People talking?

You may find journaling helpful, either as a means of making the trip itself, or as a way of reflecting on what you have imagined. You might also want to pore over old photos.

If you do decide to make a virtual pilgrimage, don't feel that you must make the journey in just one sitting. You can make the trip over a period of days, weeks, or even months.

A pilgrimage in retrospect. Another *hajj* option is to consider a pilgrimage you've already taken. Let me explain. You may have already made a trip that has all of the elements of a *hajj*, but you just didn't realize it at the time. Only later, upon deeper reflection, can you come to see that a particular experience was a sacred journey of the greatest depth, a once-in-a-lifetime pilgrimage.

Look back over your life to see if there has been a journey that, in retrospect, has the elements of a *hajj*: a visit to a site that is sacred to you because of what happened there and how it has shaped your life. If you have made such a trip, write down the story of your experience in as much detail as you can conjure. Break your pilgrimage into its stages and see what you can learn from reflecting back on them. Be deeply aware of each phase of the journey because each may hold its own significance. Ask yourself what you learned from that trip. Explore how that trip helped or hindered your mending process.

As I was preparing the material for this book, I realized that I had made such an unintentional pilgrimage much earlier than the two trips I've described. This earlier pilgrimage had, in fact, played an important role in my reconnecting with my mother. It was 1977. I hadn't seen her in eighteen years since she left me at age eight, and I hadn't communicated with her in any way for at least fifteen of those. Still, her physical absence had left me with a sense of emptiness.

The call came in the form of an article I read in *Reader's Digest* while sitting in a doctor's office. The article explained how the Social Security Administration could help you find a missing relative if you had that person's Social Security number. You could write a letter to the lost individual, put the person's name and Social Security number on the envelope, and take it to the local Social Security office. Staff there would then make an attempt to deliver the letter through the last known employer. The catch was that the Social Security staff would not tell you whether the letter had been delivered. Still, sending a letter in this way seemed like a fair gamble.

My preparation revolved around finding my mother's Social Security number. When I got home from the doctor's office, I immediately called my father to see if he might have it, but he didn't. I ran through the few details I remembered about my mom and recalled that when I was four or five years old, she had worked for a Rand McNally book factory in my hometown. Since I was planning to visit my dad, who still lived near that city, I made an appointment to visit the personnel director at Rand McNally.

On the appointed day, I sat down across the desk from the director. She pointed to an open folder on her desk and said, "I have your mother's personnel file here, but freedom of information laws prevent me from giving you the information you want." I looked at this woman for a long time. She was just doing her job. Then, with as much sternness in my voice as I could muster, I said, "Look, this is my mother. I'm going to find her one way or another whether you help me or not."

I was starting to get up to leave when the personnel director got out of her chair, walked over to the window, and looked out. It was obviously an invitation. I moved around the desk, found my mother's number on the sheet, and wrote it down. As I hurried out the door, I turned and said thank you. The personnel director continued to look out the window, but smiled.

I wish I could say that all my preparation was as successful. I wrote my letter to my mother, bringing her up to date on what had transpired in my life since she had left me. But when I returned to the Social Security office and went to hand my letter to a staff member, he gave it back to me and basically told me to get lost. I went straight to a phone and called my congressman to ask for help. A week later, the regional director of the Social Security office told me he would deal with it personally.

I did as he said and then waited for a tearful telephone call, a knock on the door, maybe a telegram saying, "I LOVE YOU STOP COMING TO SEE YOU IMMEDIATELY STOP." But that moment never arrived. A few days passed, then a week, then a month. Nothing. I thought about that letter every day. After a couple of months with no response, I gave up and went about my business, resigning myself to the idea that I had heard the last from my mother.

Four months later, I found among my bills a birthday card from my mother—with no return address. Judging by the way she worded her message, she was writing to the eight-year-old she remembered. And given that she made reference to radiation treatments, I assumed she must have cancer. But since there was no return address, the only way I could respond was to write a second letter and try to send it via the Social Security office again.

This time my letter was more direct. I pleaded for a chance to visit her.

But nothing happened. As the weeks and months went by, I began to let it all go and focused on getting on with my life. I think I turned off my feelings about her the same way I had as an eight-year-old boy.

My unexpected journey began ten months later with a phone call from a funeral home director in nearby Chicago. When he informed me that my mother was dead, I couldn't speak for several minutes. When we resumed talking, he told me that he had found my two letters in my mother's purse when he picked up her body.

In the next two hours I managed to track down my mother's sister, Helen. She contacted the other two surviving sisters, and we all met the next morning for a small, informal memorial service. I asked a minister who was a friend to officiate. There were tears, of course, especially when I saw my mother's body laid out in the cheap, potter's field casket. I didn't really recognize her face. She seemed smaller than I remembered; but then again, I was only eight when last I saw her.

When the service was over, just before the lid of the coffin was closed, I put a ring that I treasured on the cheap velvet pillow beside my mother's head. Then I touched her hand and walked away as the funeral director closed the lid. We all went to the cemetery and watched the casket lowered into the ground.

In retrospect, I can see that the arrival stage of my pilgrimage wasn't in the moment of seeing my mother's body, but rather in the events that followed the funeral. The funeral director handed me my mother's purse and the two letters it contained. Inside it were a few cosmetics, a comb, a brush, a tuft of hair, and my mother's welfare card, which bore something I had been seeking for years: her address.

I got into my car and drove to that location on the near north side of Chicago. It was a multistory, walk-up flophouse. When I arrived, I explained to the landlord that I was Mary's son. He seemed surprised that she had any survivors. I asked him if I could see my mother's apartment. It hadn't yet been rented, so he handed me the key.

I walked up the stairs and unlocked the door. On the other side was a grimy, single room. Dirty. Dusty. Smelling of urine and maybe old wine. In it were a cheap bed and a single dresser, one small bedside table, a window that had not been washed in a generation, and one straight-back chair.

When I took a step in and looked around, I was taken aback by how closely it resembled a painting by van Gogh that I had seen many times. Her room was almost exactly that painting, but without the charm. I stood there wiping my eyes and suddenly realized that, just like on a night nineteen years before, my mother had once again left me, and I was standing alone.

When I made my return home later that day, I didn't feel defeated or angry at being denied the chance to talk to her face to face. I just felt numb. At least some of my questions about my mother had been answered, even if the answers weren't the ones I wanted to hear. Putting my mother's body in the grave and seeing what she didn't want me to see at least brought a sense of closure. I had reached the end of the journey that was my relationship with her, or so I thought. As it turned out, the end of the journey was only the beginning of my exploration of my relationship with my mother. It would take years of therapy to reach the point where I could acknowledge the fact that, whatever her problems, when my mother had responsibility for my care, she did the best she could. It took me an even longer period of time to forgive her for what she couldn't do. But I have. That was a major milestone in my mending.

FACING THE PROVERBIAL DRAGON

As I warned earlier in the chapter, making a pilgrimage may be the most difficult and painful of the tools you explore in this book. Making a *hajj* to the place where your brokenness began is strong medicine. But strong medicine can have very powerful positive effects in your life if you are willing to endure emotional discomfort. Revisiting the scenes of your brokenness is strong medicine that you can use in your mending process.

One of the benefits of such a pilgrimage is that it offers you the opportunity to check your memories of events and see if the reality of the places match what you recall. Were things as bad as you remember? Worse? Better?

A pilgrimage may give you some sense of closure, as it did for me. Be aware, however, that closure is not a guarantee. Closure, however, can be an outcome of your willingness to go back and face places that remind you of tremendous pain, while also reminding you that you survived that pain.

A *hajj* can also be an opportunity to figuratively return the pain to its rightful owner, a declaration, if you will, that you will no longer carry it.

A pilgrimage is also a chance to face the proverbial dragon and say to its face, "Look! I am here! You did what you did, and you did not defeat me! As a vital part of my life journey, I come to acknowledge you, even honor you, for in spite of the pain you caused, or maybe because of it, I have come to cultivate new strengths and resources, to be the me I am today."

If you think a pilgrimage could help you mend your brokenness, take some time to journal about the challenges, problems, and opportunities that a *hajj* might offer you. It is important to be aware that the pilgrimage you plan may ultimately not hold the meaning you were seeking. Or it may take you to a destination that surprises you.

Be open also to unexpected opportunities to make sacred journeys that present themselves from time to time. Take advantage of them, if you can. Sometimes you may consciously choose to make a pilgrimage, but at other times a pilgrimage may choose you. Wherever your pilgrimage takes you—whether it is a literal trip or a virtual journey—you can return with new eyes that help you continue to find the meaning in your experience of brokenness.

6

LABYRINTH

Moving On with Your Brokenness

AN ANCIENT PRACTICE

While on a trip to northern New Mexico some years ago, visiting the Ghost Ranch Presbyterian Conference Center, I discovered the power of the labyrinth. If you know the desert paintings of Georgia O'Keeffe, you know a little of the Ghost Ranch setting because that's where O'Keeffe lived and painted. I spent my time at the ranch mostly in solitude, walking among the scrub brush and rocks and solitary flowers, enjoying the way the hue of the already multicolored mesas changed continuously throughout the day, from sunrise to the sun's final dip below the mountain to the west.

On one of my daily explorations, I passed by a labyrinth marked out in the gray dusty sand by mountain stones the size of ostrich eggs. It was late afternoon when I made the discovery, and I was on my way to explore a wooded area at the back of the ranch's box canyon, so I paused only for a moment. But I made a mental note to read a bit about labyrinths and return the next day.

At that point, the labyrinth was a puzzle to me, both literally and figuratively. I certainly had heard of the idea, and several of my friends had told me that labyrinths played an important role in their spiritual lives, but I couldn't say that I really knew what a labyrinth was. That evening I found Lauren Artress's book *Walking a Sacred Path: Rediscovering the Labyrinth as a Spiritual Practice* in the Ghost Ranch library and read it from cover to cover. It was a book that would put me on a path of making the labyrinth a core part of my spiritual practice as I dealt with my brokenness.

Walking the labyrinth is one of the most ancient of spiritual practices. According to Artress, who is the founder of Veriditas, the World-Wide Labyrinth Project, there is evidence of labyrinth designs on pottery, tablets, and tiles dating as far back as five thousand years ago. The basic pattern of the labyrinth reflects spirals found in nature, such as a snail shell, a whirlpool, or the inner ear, and its prominent feature is that there is only one way into the center, with the return following the same path out.

Nearly every major religious tradition has a labyrinth-like symbol. For Native Americans, it is found in the Medicine Wheel. For Celts, it is found in the Never Ending Circle. In the Jewish mystical tradition of Kabbalah, it is found in the Tree of Life. For Tibetan monks, it is found in mandala sand paintings.

In recent years, there has been a renaissance in the use of the labyrinth as a meditation tool, across religious and secular boundaries, springing up in centers of worship, public parks, retreat centers—even in private backyards. What people are discovering is that walking the labyrinth is a way to involve the whole body in the meditation experience. It is a physical form of prayer that quiets the mind and encourages insight.

If you've never walked a labyrinth before, when you come to the entrance, it looks as if you are entering a maze. However, unlike a maze where you have to figure out which way to turn (so you don't get trapped or lost), the labyrinth has only one path. All you need to do is follow the twists and turns of that path, and you will come to the center, the goal of your journey. Then, all you need to do is follow the same path outward, and it will return you safely to the beginning.

You can get the idea of how this works simply by "walking" your fingers on this drawing of one of the most ancient and simple labyrinth designs:

A Symbol for the Journey

The many twists and turns of the circuitous path of the labyrinth make it an especially appropriate symbol for those of us who experience brokenness. If your struggle is at all like mine, the very moment you feel as though you have made some progress in mending your brokenness, something occurs that puts you right back in the midst of your pain. With the labyrinth, however, though the path meanders and seems to take you away from your goal, the promise is that if you continue the journey, you will reach your goal. It may take longer than you expect or want, and it may contain some surprising twists and turns, but the goal is within reach. A labyrinth by its very nature assures you that no matter what you do, you won't get lost. It assures you that if you keep on moving, you will arrive at the center, and once you have, you will always find your way back.

Walking the labyrinth can help you think about the very real ways that your journey toward mending has its own twists and turns. The physical movement becomes a spiritual reflection that can help you move on with your life while you are mending, rather than postponing life until you reach the goal of a "cure."

At a spiritual level, walking the labyrinth can be a physical form of prayer. Presbyterian spiritual leader Kris Haig put it this way in an article she wrote on labyrinths for *Hungryhearts Magazine*:

> You can ... "know" things while meditatively walking the circuitous path of a ... labyrinth which you can't know sitting still. The very action of walking serves to still our thoughts, allowing space for God amid the usually jam packed confines of our minds. The rhythm of walking is conducive to prayerful contemplation. The unpredictability of the labyrinth's twists and turns helps us to relinquish our need to feel "in control" and to acknowledge our dependence on God. The certainty of reaching the center inspires us to trust in God's providence. All of these things can serve to draw us into a genuine experience of prayer—of allowing our hearts to lay "open to God." (Volume VIII, Number 2, Summer 2000)

When I took my first few steps into the Ghost Ranch labyrinth, I didn't know what to expect, but I was surprised when my steps brought me in no time at all to the very edge of the labyrinth's center. I had to laugh. That was quick! However, once I got to that point, even though I could see my goal, I could also see that there was no way into the center from where I stood. Instead, the path took me on a meandering stroll that led me away from the center's edge almost back to the beginning. I had to smile again: it was just like my spiritual journey. Every time I encounter a new spiritual idea or the latest meditative practice, I want it instantly to solve all of my problems and make me a perfectly spiritual person. It's what I call "light switch" spirituality.

What I came to discover is that this ancient tool of the labyrinth offers us a uniquely modern way to deal with our brokenness, both as we walk its spiraling path and as we work with it as a symbol for our journey. There are several reasons why the labyrinth is such a powerful tool to use on the spiritual journey toward mending:

Walking the labyrinth reminds us that there are no quick or easy paths to solving our problems. The "trick" of the labyrinth is that just at the moment when we think we have reached the center, we find ourselves back at the beginning. And, of course, that's exactly the situation with brokenness. Just when we think we have everything figured out, we may find ourselves right back where we started. When we are especially weary of the misery of being our broken selves, we may feel desperate to find anything that will make us feel instantly okay, but the labyrinth's subtle but insistent message is to pursue the journey. The goal is further down the path, and we will get there if we keep on moving.

Walking the labyrinth teaches us patience. I can still remember the first time I walked that labyrinth in New Mexico. I had looked at it the night before, and from a quick glance, had judged that it would probably take me about five minutes of slow walking to reach the center and another five to return to the entrance. If I spent five minutes in the center, I figured I could complete the total process in about fifteen minutes. When I actually walked the labyrinth the next day, I discovered that, moving at a normal pace, it took me twenty minutes to navigate the many turns and movements in and out before I reached the center. Added to that, I chose to spend another twenty minutes in the center, and the outbound trip took another twenty. Altogether, it took an hour to complete the labyrinth—that's four times longer than I had thought. I couldn't help but see the parallels to my mending journey.

Because the twists and turns of the labyrinth intentionally slow us down, they teach us one of the most valuable attitudes in dealing with brokenness: patience, the slow steadiness that it takes to move one step at a time toward our goal of mending. The circuitous path of the labyrinth is a reminder that when the process of finding our hidden wholeness is taking longer than we think it "should," when it feels as if we're moving away from our center rather than toward it, each step is actually bringing us closer. Having the mindful patience to keep on walking mirrors the spiritual practice necessary to stay on the journey.

Walking the labyrinth brings us to a safe place where we can leave our spiritual and emotional baggage behind. I'll be frank: there are times on the journey to mending when pain and anguish become almost too much to bear. The center of the labyrinth provides a wonderful safe place to set these hurts down for a moment. Reaching the center of the labyrinth symbolizes reaching the core of our problem, and if we can leave some of the hurt we carry around with us behind, we may find it easier to live with who we are, just as we are. Our pain may return, but we can give ourselves the relief of letting it go, if even only for a few minutes.

Walking the labyrinth is a reminder of hope. We may wish for a journey to wholeness that takes us on a straight path, but that hope flies in the face of the labyrinth's first truth: in leading us to its center, the labyrinth spins us back and forth through dozens of switchbacks. What could be more representative of the spiritual journey that presents daily challenges that constantly force us to change direction? Sometimes we move closer to our goal; other times we make choices that seem to take us farther away from where we want to be. The gift of the labyrinth lies in its second truth: all the while we are moving ever closer to the center. Even though, at times, we seem to find ourselves almost back at the beginning, if we trust the labyrinth path, the journey itself will lead us to its (and our) center.

Walking the labyrinth teaches us to pay attention to the process. How we reach the goal is as important as the goal itself. If we are patient, we can begin to trust the process. As we move back and forth on the labyrinth paths, in and out, we can benefit by being mindful of how similar this may be to our own journey toward mending. Our journey also has twists and turns; we make progress and suffer setbacks. Still, if we trust that the mending path will lead us to our goal, as the meandering walkway of the labyrinth does, we can proceed with both the symbolic and the actual journeys in peace and confidence.

Walking the labyrinth gives us a physical form of meditation to add to our more sedentary practices. Many, if not most, meditation techniques call us to be sedentary. In contrast, I think of walking the labyrinth as a form of low-impact walking meditation, similar in a way to the experience of Tai Chi. Walking the labyrinth with its twists and turns provides a gentle way to exercise not only our spirits and minds but our bodies as well. If you have suffered emotional or spiritual distress, you know the physical symptoms: a tightness in your face or other parts of your body, headaches or stomach discomfort, physical tension and tiredness. You probably also know that physical exercise is one of the best antidotes for depression or stress. One of the extra benefits of walking the labyrinth is that it gets our blood coursing through our veins, and it stretches our tension-filled muscles.

Walking the labyrinth teaches us that we have many opportunities for mending. One of the great things about a labyrinth is that we can walk it over and over, whenever we need it. This is a very important factor when you consider that most of us who are broken also make our mistakes over and over again. The labyrinth gives us someplace to go with our pain again and again. And each time, the labyrinth patiently stands ready to welcome us, to teach us that we can begin again. As you mend your brokenness, I encourage you to walk the labyrinth whenever you need a comforting reminder that your journey is going to take you where you need to be and return you safely home.

A Practical Method for Walking a Labyrinth

Obviously, the first thing you will need to do is *find* a labyrinth! I'll say more later about possible alternatives, but I suggest you start by looking for a labyrinth near you. Labyrinths have become very popular, and they can often be found at churches in large or medium-sized cities, or at retreat centers. An especially helpful tool in finding a labyrinth is the World-Wide Labyrinth Locator (sponsored by The Labyrinth Society and Veriditas). You can go online at labyrinthlocator.com and type in your location to find out what labyrinths might be available to you. You might be surprised at what you discover.

Once you've found a labyrinth you can visit, it is helpful to consider how you might best use this spiritual tool to help in mending your brokenness. I suggest following the same five steps that I outline for making a pilgrimage: the call, the preparation, the journey, the arrival, and the return.

Step 1: The Call

Even though I have access to a nearby labyrinth on a daily basis, I don't have a regular schedule for walking it. I usually go to the labyrinth when something prompts me to seek its solace. I sometimes walk the labyrinth when I am carrying a problem or an issue in my heart that I am wrestling with. On other occasions I walk it because I am feeling tense, stressed, or overwhelmed. Sometimes

I walk the labyrinth because I am carrying with me a pain or a problem that is confronting someone else. If someone I know is having a problem, or needs spiritual comforting, I may invite that person to walk the labyrinth with me.

While you may feel drawn to walk the labyrinth at specific times of intensity, I'm not at all suggesting that you need a specific reason to walk the labyrinth. Its beauty, power, and comfort are enriching no matter what your circumstances are. You might want to walk the labyrinth periodically, perhaps once a month, or every other week. But do keep your heart open to what the path might call to your attention as you move along the twisting course of the labyrinth.

Step 2: The Preparation

Before you enter the labyrinth, take a moment to prepare. If you have felt a call to make this particular walk, review in your mind what specific problem or need is prompting your walk. See if you can articulate it in a sentence or two. You might want to write your thoughts on a piece of paper that you can leave in the center of the labyrinth, if there is an appropriate place to do so. (Please be careful not to litter). Decide if you want to take anything else along as a physical symbol of your brokenness, or the place where it began, to leave in the center of the labyrinth to represent what you are leaving behind. (It is helpful if such a symbolic object is natural and biodegradable, especially if the labyrinth is outdoors.) You could compose some words to speak when you reach the labyrinth's center, or perhaps bring along a poem or song by someone else that is meaningful to you that you could recite or sing.

Before you enter the labyrinth, take a moment to calm and center yourself as you would if you were beginning a time of sitting meditation. Adopt an attitude of openness to ideas or impressions that might come to you on your walk. If you are walking the labyrinth without a specific call or purpose, you may want to take a moment to prepare yourself by going through the steps of consciously relaxing each part of your body.

Step 3: The Journey

Because we are so busy, we have a tendency to rush through everything we do, so we can mark it off our "to-do" list and move on to the next task. This is not the way of the labyrinth. Walking the circuitous paths invites slowing down, taking your time, paying attention to your steps and to your breathing. It is a time to notice the small details: your breathing, your movements back and forth, the sounds, smells, and textures around you. As the path takes you closer to the center, ponder how this journey inward relates to the issue or problem with which you are wrestling. What parallels do you see?

Step 4: The Arrival

When you reach the labyrinth's center, I urge you to stay for at least as long as it took you to slowly walk the labyrinth's inward path. Sit or stand quietly. Try to remain still, completely motionless. How does that stillness feel? Consider performing a small ritual to mark your arrival and to honor anything you are literally or metaphorically leaving behind.

A ritual is simply an outward physical manifestation of an inward process, a creative act that has an intention, and a beginning, a middle, and an end. It may have words, actions, props, sounds, or movements. Some of the best rituals include elements that involve all of our senses—sight, hearing, smell, touch, and taste. For example, if you have brought with you a physical symbol of your brokenness, you could create a special movement when you place your object in the labyrinth's center so that your actions reflect your thoughts and feelings. If you have brought some words, a poem, or a song with you, use your time at the labyrinth's center to read or sing your reflection. Your ritual might include the burning of incense (if appropriate) to represent the invocation of spirit. Consider composing an opening and a closing prayer, or other spiritual expression, to mark the beginning and ending of your ritual. Finally, don't forget to pay attention to the sense of touch in your ritual. Not just the texture of the object you carry and perhaps leave, but also the temperature of the air, the feel of a breeze on your face, and any other physical sensation that draws your attention.

After you have completed your ritual, turn your attention toward the outward journey. Before you start out, review what you have been thinking about during your inward walk and your time in the center. Is there a different attitude or a new idea that you wish to carry with you on the outward journey?

Step 5: The Return

On your walk back toward the labyrinth's entrance, I suggest a practice of turning attention away from yourself and toward the needs and problems of others. You might want to use the idea of *tonglen* from chapter 3—with each in-breath, take in the pain of the sufferer; with each out-breath, send out goodness and joy. Making that connection with others can help ease your pain and remind you that you are not alone on your journey.

Just as a pilgrimage is not complete without some consideration of the meaning of the journey, so too is it important to take some time in prayer or journaling to ponder your experience, noting what you have learned in your mind and in your heart.

ॐ

There is one other suggestion I want to add here, and this has to do with encountering others. If you walk a labyrinth, you will probably pass other people along the way, coming or going. You may be on the way into the center while someone is on the way out. Some people find this experience annoying because it causes them to break their concentration, disturbing their meditative attitude.

I want to suggest that this encountering of others can serve as a symbol of what happens on the spiritual journey. You may be fully involved in your journey, heading toward your center, dealing with a particular personal pain. Or you may be on your way back, focused on returning to the world in a new way. There, in the midst of the path, something or someone presents you with a situation or a problem that you need to stop and address. It may make your journey longer, or different than the one you had planned.

Encountering others on the labyrinth path reminds us that even when things don't quite work out as we planned, or our mending process is interrupted or delayed, the path always awaits us. We can walk, and rest, at our own pace. There is room for more than just our pain and brokenness on the path, and we do have companions on the journey. The point is not that we need "ideal" circumstances to mend, but that we can always keep on moving toward mending from our brokenness.

Labyrinth Alternatives and Suggestions

If you are not able to find a labyrinth near you, there are a number of ways you can engage in the labyrinth's spiritual benefits. One way is to bring creative visualization to the process. A quick search of the web using the terms "online labyrinth" will provide you with a list of sites where you can have a virtual labyrinth experience by moving a cursor along a path on the screen. Some of these sites have relaxing music or inspirational texts to help you focus your mind and heart on the process. If you don't have access to a computer, you can find books in most public libraries that contain pictures of labyrinths. Use a stylus or similar device to trace your way through a labyrinth on paper, using the five steps I've suggested for walking a physical labyrinth. It is also possible to purchase or make small labyrinths. Labyrinths printed on cloth can be used indoors or outdoors. Instructions for creating your own labyrinth on a floor, in a garden, or in some other outdoor setting are readily available. Labyrinths can also be mowed into fields of grass.

You might also consider using the labyrinth in conjunction with other spiritual tools introduced in this book. I find that I use the labyrinth to work on questions or issues that come up in other spiritual practices that I am using to cope with my sense of brokenness. If, for example, I am doing *Lectio Divina* with some aspect of my life story, I find it very healing to carry the details of that story with me in my head and heart as I walk to the labyrinth's center. When I reach the center, I savor my story for a while, then I make a symbolic gesture to indicate that, for the time being, I am going to leave the story and all of the emotions it raises behind. Sometimes I do this by touching my slightly cupped hand to the ground, as though I were releasing a baby bird. Then I walk back to the world with an openness to make new stories. This is one way I recover my hidden wholeness.

If I have been wrestling with a particularly tough recurrence of "emotional sludge," and I am using *maitri* to get in touch with the source of the pain, I sometimes take that particular pain with me on a walk through the labyrinth. I find that experiencing my pain within the symbolic geography of twists and turns is a powerful reminder that this emotion is part of a much larger journey. Sitting with it in the center of the labyrinth reminds me that this pain is paradoxically part of my hidden wholeness. And walking from the center of the labyrinth back to its entranceway reminds me that I am reentering a world that begs me to do something about the pain of others through the practice of *tonglen*, by feeling a sense of solidarity with others who are suffering.

As Lauren Artress states so beautifully in *Walking a Sacred Path: Rediscovering the Labyrinth as a Spiritual Practice*, "Generally there are three stages to the walk: releasing on the way in, receiving in the center and returning; that is, taking back out into the world that which you have received. There is no right way or wrong way to walk a labyrinth. Use the labyrinth in any way that meets what you need."

I hope you will take these words to heart and discover for yourself that the road to mending can be lived and learned in the simple experience of a labyrinth.

A Sacramental Journey to Hidden Wholeness

One recent summer I led a weeklong retreat on "A Spirituality for Brokenness" at Ghost Ranch, where I had first encountered the labyrinth. As one of the meditation exercises during the week, I asked the participants to explore the geography of the ranch and find a place that spoke to them about their feeling of brokenness. I asked them to spend some time there every day and to bring back a physical object from that location that mirrored their feeling of brokenness. Some chose stones, others chose leaves, still others chose feathers. At least one chose sand.

For the concluding ritual of the retreat, all of the participants came together to walk the ranch's labyrinth. The first person who entered its center spontaneously placed the symbol of her brokenness in the dust and then waited for the next person to arrive. The next person stayed, too, and placed the symbol of his brokenness beside the first. One by one, we filled the heart of the labyrinth with our symbols and our bodies until all seventeen of us were present. We joined arms and simultaneously broke into tears.

We felt no urgency about leaving the center of the labyrinth or, for that matter, the sense of brokenness that we were symbolically leaving behind. After about ten minutes, we walked out of the center single file, retracing our steps, plunging back into the twists and turns, knowing that we had found a way to leave our sense of brokenness behind, knowing that our symbols might be found and picked up by others who themselves were walking the labyrinth as a way of struggling to find a hidden wholeness at the center of their brokenness.

The first person reached the starting point and moved out of the labyrinth, waiting for the rest of us. It took twenty minutes for the last walker to reach the entrance. We exchanged only smiles. No words. We didn't need verbal language to express the journey that continued inside us. Each of us knew that the feeling of brokenness, the "embarrassment of being you," would come back from time to time. But we also knew that each time it did, we had tools to deal with our pain and struggle. If the pain and anguish returned a thousand times, we could deal with it a thousand times. For us as a group, this was a moment of recovering some of our hidden wholeness simply by accepting ourselves just as we were, not in spite of our brokenness but because of it.

I think this is a little of what Artress means in her description of the labyrinth as "a watering hole for the spirit and a mirror of the soul." The labyrinth reflects our soul's winding journey to wholeness and the promise of arriving at the center—no matter how many twists and turns we make—where we can lay down our burdens and renew ourselves for the journey onward.

7

THE YOGA OF CREATIVITY

Transcending Your Brokenness

TURNING LEAD INTO GOLD

Brokenness can get very heavy. And it is when life begins to feel like lead that it is helpful to remember there are spiritual tools available that can turn our lead into gold. Creative expression is one of those tools.

When we make creative expression part of an ongoing spiritual discipline, we embrace a tool that can help us deal with our sense of brokenness in a sustainable way. In earlier chapters we have explored tools that can be used once or multiple times. But here I want to focus on an approach that will provide bread for the journey, bread that will nourish us as we move toward mending, bread that will help us develop a sustainable spiritual path: the "yoga of creativity."

Most of us know the idea of yoga as a sort of spiritual exercise program. And that it is. But our Hindu brothers and sisters also refer to creativity as a yoga, a discipline, or a pathway to the Transcendent.

Before I talk more about yoga, and about how this specific type of yoga, creativity, can help in the mending of brokenness, I want to talk about the religion within which the concept of yoga was born. I would like to clear up a common misconception about Hinduism. Many people believe that Hindus worship many gods. In fact, even though Hindus do identify an almost countless number of gods, the most enlightened Hindus I've met see these gods as different manifestations of one true transcendent being. Often these gods represent different aspects of God (divine, transcendent reality). In the Hindu trinity of Brahma, Vishnu, and Shiva, for example, the first is creator, the second, preserver, and the third, destroyer. Among the literally thousands of gods (or manifestations of Brahma) in Hinduism, multiple beings figuratively represent virtually every aspect or trait of the Divine.

In a similar way, the Hindus understand perhaps better than those of us who practice Western religions that there are countless ways to approach God. Hindus recognize that, because each of us is unique, each of us will find different ways to the Divine. Hindus give us new eyes to see that there are many different pathways to the Transcendent.

I think this is one of Hinduism's greatest gifts, because it takes away the shame and sense of failure that some of us feel about our spiritual practices when they don't seem to "work" for us. I can't tell you the number of times I have encountered people who claim to have a unique (sometimes "the best" or "the only") path to God. For some, the path might be salvation, or a creed, or meditation. For others, the path leads through serving the poor, or an in-depth study of scriptures or music, or a campaign for or against a belief or behavior. The problem is that if someone else is seeking God through a different path, the implication is that they are doing it "wrong." That doesn't allow room for very many differences.

The Hindus freely embrace that no one path to God is necessarily better than the others. They begin by positing four yogas, or disciplines, for connecting with the Transcendent:

> *Karma Yoga*: the yoga of service; embracing
>   work with right intentions.
> *Bhakti Yoga*: the yoga of devotion; absolute
>   devotion and love of God.
> *Jnana Yoga*: the yoga of knowledge and self-
>   inquiry; devoted study.
> *Raja Yoga*: a yoga integrating all the forms; disci-
>   plined control of the body and mind.

A fundamental aspect of each yoga is that it is not only a path but also a discipline that requires ongoing, daily attention in order to connect us with the Divine. Such a discipline calls for the commitment, attention, and regularity that can turn this spiritual practice into bread for the ongoing journey toward mending.

DEVELOPING A SUSTAINABLE SPIRITUAL PATH

Several years ago I spent some time with a young Indian spiritual master and musician named Russill Paul, who helped me see that carrying a discipline, a practice, a *yoga* into my daily life would provide me with something missing from my mending from brokenness: a sustainable spiritual path. Moreover, his use of personal expression as a special form of yoga unlocked for me a closed door that had kept me from experiencing my personal creativity as an ongoing part of my spiritual life.

In his book *The Yoga of Sound: Tapping the Hidden Power of Music and Chant*, Russill presents the idea of "the yoga of sound." Russill grew up in India, and one of his parents was Hindu, the other Christian. For some years Russill was part of a Christian monastic community called Shantivanam Ashram, led by Bede Griffiths, an extraordinary Catholic monk who combined the spirituality of Christianity with the spiritual disciplines of Hinduism.

At Shantivanam, Russill was profoundly influenced by the practice of chanting mantras (repeating sacred words over and over) to connect to the Divine. This led him to focus on the practice of *Nada Yoga,* or literally, "sound as a form of yoga." *Nada* in Sanskrit is a term that has existed in Indian spirituality for several thousand years, and it refers to sound, pitch, drone, stream, flow, or current of sound. Russill's "yoga of sound" is a way of using the voice, breath, and movement for healing and empowerment. It involves the body, mind, and spirit in a way that brings a state of peacefulness—even bliss—both potent antidotes to the pain and anguish of brokenness.

My experience of meeting Russill and taking part in his workshops led me to begin exploring other ways that creative expression can connect us with the Transcendent, while at the same time addressing my brokenness.

The most important aspects of what I learned from Russill were hidden within what he was teaching. The first was the fact that, even though the mantras we were chanting were created by someone else, we were using our own voices, our own music, and our own creativity to express and explore them. The second insight I had was that the twin concepts of discipline and practice were missing from my spiritual life. As I spent time with what I had learned from Russill, I saw more and more clearly that undertaking creative expression—a "yoga of creativity," if you will—on a regular schedule would provide me the outlet I needed to mend my soul.

THE GIFTS OF CREATIVE EXPRESSION

One of the greatest gifts of creativity is that it helps us transcend ourselves and the sense of brokenness we feel. Being creative delivers us from the realm of fact and reality into the world of imagination, a world where anything can happen. When we are using our creativity to express and work with our brokenness, we are taking the opportunity to move our brokenness outside ourselves, if even for a few moments.

One of the wonderful things about using disciplined creativity as a spiritual practice to deal with brokenness is that there are almost limitless tools available to us: chanting, singing, painting, quilt making, dancing, drama, poetry, filmmaking, photography, dreamwork, writing fiction, keeping a visual journal (or a written journal), and much more.

Unfortunately, many people run into a roadblock when it comes to the idea of being "creative." I've noticed that when I invite people in a workshop to do something creative, many seem ready to head for the exit. Many of us don't think of ourselves as creative; we think that creativity is for someone else. This has been true for me over the years. Even when I was taking a printmaking class as part of my work for my master's in fine arts at the University of Alabama (which, by many people's criteria, would already identify me as a "creative type"), I frequently addressed my fellow printmaking students as, "You artists." Finally, one of the students said to me, "Why do you address us as, 'You artists'? You are an artist, too."

That was an empowering moment for me. I saw that we can all be artists, or more broadly speaking, all of us not only *can* be, but *are* creative. We just need to learn to recognize when and how we are being creative. The fact is, we almost can't help doing things that are creative! Take a blank sheet of paper and a pen or pencil and sit down at a table or desk. Begin randomly making dots on the paper. Continue this process for a few minutes. After a while, you'll probably begin to see a pattern of some kind in the dots. Your mind's eye looks at things in an interpretive way. What you see is not what someone else will see. Simply by being yourself, you are being creative.

Creativity really isn't all that complicated. It is, fundamentally, the ability to see new possibilities in things. Catholic priest and yoga instructor Thomas Ryan, in his book *Soul Fire: Accessing Your Creativity* (SkyLight Paths), writes, "Creativity asks us, in the midst of the contrarieties of daily living, to believe there are new possibilities out there, to loosen our control and take more risks, to let life unfold. The creative process ... is about rearranging *us*, opening us up emotionally, exposing us to surprising presences, and coming up with new combinations of possibilities."

Creativity in any form can be a powerful spiritual tool to open up possibilities, ease the pain of brokenness (and perhaps experience joy), and connect to the Transcendent. Your yoga of creative expression can become a spiritual practice that is an ongoing, sustainable way of tending your hurts and furthering your mending process. Here are a few ways such a yoga can help:

Creative expression can give you a new perspective. Creativity affords you the ability to look at your brokenness from a different perspective and then return it to its place in your heart in a different, perhaps more endurable form. Expressing pain in a painting or poem, musically, or in dance, gives you a chance to step back and gain some distance from your suffering. Creative expression can also bring a sense of accomplishment, because you have found a way to represent what you feel.

Creative expression can ease your sense of disconnection. Spiritually, transcending yourself connects you with the Transcendent. That may sound a bit strange, but think about it. God, or the Transcendent, is a being that goes beyond the everyday, beyond what appears to be reality. When you transcend or move beyond yourself and your own pain, you mirror the concept of transcendence as it is expressed in the idea of God.

An interesting phenomenon happens in the process of creative expression: when you engage in the creative process, you can "lose" yourself—or, more accurately, move beyond yourself—and become part of the process. If you lose yourself for a few minutes, you can often also leave behind your focus on your own pain so you can concentrate on enjoyable parts of your life, as well as the needs of others. That moving beyond yourself is a form of transcendence.

Creative expression is empowering. Virtually every religion has a creation myth in which, broadly speaking, something is created out of nothing. In many of these myths, the creation is accomplished by God or the most powerful being in the world. So, too, when you are feeling that one or more aspects of your life is out of control or beyond your control, creative expression can empower you to express your feelings in a way that you control, a way that is neither right nor wrong, acceptable nor unacceptable, clear nor confused. It is simply what you have chosen to communicate.

Creative expression is a way of making your invisible interior visible. Before you have words to express your feelings, you may have a sense of shape, color, movement, or sound that can nonverbally express your feelings. Finding a creative form that moves straight to expression, without judging or moralizing, allows for an expression of a gritty reality that communicates what you are experiencing in a way that words cannot. What you put out in the world is reflective of at least part of your interior world.

I want to add a special word, though, about making your feelings visible: if you have a fear of other people seeing or, even more important, judging the product of your creativity, remember that your creativity is *your* expression. You don't have to share your process or product with anyone but yourself. If at any point you do decide to share, that will be its own experience, from which you might gain many insights. But, for now, I'm talking about creative expression that is simply an extension of the unique being you are. There is no need to apply evaluative terms such as "good" or "bad." There is no right or wrong way to do it, no competition.

Creative expression can be an outlet for your feelings when they become overwhelming. One of the great challenges of brokenness is the loneliness of the pain, the sense of emotions being bottled up. The pain of brokenness can be intense at times, and if you can't find a way to express it, it can overwhelm you. But if you can find a way to express it, to represent it, you can begin to see that your pain isn't infinite. It won't kill you or destroy you. Creative expression provides an opportunity to uncork the bottle and "let it all out" through painting, dancing, acting, making music, or another creative tool. These venues also give you a healthy alternative to lashing out at someone or something.

One of the most powerful examples of creative expression of brokenness is the artwork of Vincent van Gogh. I like to say that if you've ever seen one of van Gogh's paintings, you don't need to read a biography of him. Everything you need to know about van Gogh is right there on the canvas: his pain, his passionate love of the world, and his madness. It is almost as though van Gogh couldn't help revealing himself when he painted. His work is one of the best examples I can think of to illustrate the power of creative expression.

Of course, Vincent's life story doesn't have a happy ending. His painting and drawing gave him some joy, but his despair overwhelmed him. I wonder if Vincent's story would have ended more happily if he had continued his creative work but had been able to access the services of an art therapist. Since art therapy didn't exist when he was alive, we will never know. I'll say more about this later, but I do want to add here that sometimes creative expression on its own isn't enough to be truly a mending experience. Some things may surface that would be good to share with a close friend or counseling professional. As you explore your creative outlets, be aware that these expressions are your brokenness made visible, and you will need to treat them with tender care.

Creativity as a Spiritual Practice

Before you consider what forms of creative expression you might want to explore to help in the mending of your brokenness, I want to be very clear about one thing: even though the yoga of creativity is a spiritual practice, it does not need to address a specifically religious theme. Spiritual experiences are not limited to religious activities. Have you ever looked at a painting, for example, that gave you goosebumps? Or seen a photograph of a child that brought quick tears or touched something deep in your soul? Or watched someone dance or listened to someone play the piano, and felt a rush of awe? Have you ever read a poem that expressed exactly how you felt? Or viewed a film that seemed to detail the key themes of your life story?

These *are* spiritual experiences. And in much the same way that spiritual experiences are not limited to "religious" experiences, creative experiences are not limited to "artistic" experiences. The range of creativity is as unlimited as creativity itself. Below, I offer a few suggestions for creative expression that I hope will help spark your imagination. Rather than use the standard terms of "art," "dance", "music," and "drama," I prefer more open-ended terms: bodily expression, visual expression, sound expression, and experiential expression. While you might not consider your-self a dancer, you can still explore bodily movement as a form of creative expression!

As you peruse the list of suggestions, see what forms of expression appeal to you. Consider making that expression your spiritual practice for the day. Or you might want to experiment with several forms of creativity and make a list of the ones that seem to work best for you. Then begin creating for yourself a plan for using these creativity tools (along with the spiritual tools we have explored in previous chapters) to develop a well-planned, disciplined spiritual practice.

Bodily Expression

Free movement. You could start with a simple practice of just letting your body move. Clear out some space in your liv-ing room or in your backyard. Stand still for a moment, with your eyes closed if you like, and then simply allow your body to start moving. Let your body express itself in whatever way it wishes. Afterward, journal about what your body felt like before, during, and after the experience. Using free movement to express your brokenness provides a tangible, visceral way of expressing your hurt that can make concrete what seems to be abstract. Your hurt is real, and expressing it physically can help you own your hurt and feel comfortable with communicating about it.

A dance about brokenness. If you'd like to try something a little more challenging, consider creating a dance about brokenness. There is a famous quote attributed to the jazz musician Thelonius Monk: "Talking about music is like dancing about architecture." The line "dancing about architecture" is a compelling image. Why not a "dance about brokenness"? You could start with a series of movements that express how you feel about your brokenness. (Be careful to choose movements or positions that are not dangerous or physically harmful.) Then create another dance that expresses how you would *like* to feel. Finally, think about Monk's comment, "dancing about architecture," and create a dance to describe the place most closely connected with your brokenness.

Journal about each of these experiences, and the feelings and ideas they provoke. Did your perspective of your brokenness shift? Can you see or understand something about your story of brokenness that was hidden before?

Visual Expression

Free drawing. Take a blank piece of paper and, using a pencil, pen, marker, crayon, or whatever drawing tools you have available, begin moving your drawing instrument on the paper. Let your hand move in any direction or pattern it chooses. Do this for just a few minutes. When you are done, place your drawing in your sacred space where you can contemplate it and honor the wholeness and holiness of its expression.

A visual journal. Consider keeping a visual journal or diary. Get a blank book (or perhaps make your own) in which to respond each day to the events, feelings, and ideas that have filled the previous twenty-four hours. Use pencils, markers, paints, and other materials (you might also want to include pictures clipped from newspapers or magazines) to make a visual record of your day.

Try developing your own visual vocabulary of colors, lines, shapes, and images and then associating these with your feelings or ideas. What color would represent sadness? What shape would you use to convey anger? What image could represent a success in your day? Be imaginative. Be counterintuitive. Do something different from what would be "logical." Blue, for example, is a typical color to represent sadness or depression. What would happen if you used yellow or orange? Draw in your journal (drawing skill not necessary!). Scribble. Paint swatches of color. Clip ads, pictures, cartoons, or words from newspapers, magazines, or flyers you receive in the mail and glue them onto your page. Stain the page with coffee or tea. Paste in a leaf or other natural item.

Make a visual record every day for at least a month as part of your spiritual practice. If you can't make an entry every day for a month, make entries whenever you can until they add up to at least a month. If you look through its pages from time to time, such a visual record can give you new insights about how your brokenness is expressing itself in your day-to-day life, what you may be doing to cope, and whether or not your coping mechanisms are helping you mend.

Three-dimensional expression. Look around your home, garage, basement, shed, office, or classroom and gather together cast-aside objects that in some way communicate to you a sense of wholeness in the face of brokenness. Let these items speak to you; let them choose you. You might consider objects that are broken, damaged, outdated, or incomplete, but you may want to go beyond the more usual objects. What might have a hidden sense of brokenness? What might suggest wholeness?

Once you have gathered an array of meaningful objects, find a board, box, or other base on which to combine these items into a sculptural collage. Spend some meditation time gazing at your creation. If you spend some time with it, as you did with your story of brokenness in the *Lectio Divina* chapter, you may find that your assemblage provides new or deeper insights into the nature of your brokenness, its sources, and what might help you continue to mend.

Pages of a life. Consider creating a scrapbook in which you document the life you *would* have lived if you had had your choice. You could start by visiting junk shops and flea markets to find items that people typically keep in scrapbooks, such as photos, invitations, awards, birth certificates, wedding memorabilia, and so forth. As you explore such memorabilia, let the items you find help you create the story of a life you haven't lived. What would such a life be like? (If you'd like to do a shorter version of this, look through your junk mail for an image that represents to you a life you might like to have lived.) Creating such a story might give you the opportunity to visualize yourself in an unbroken state. You might want to consider comparing your real life story to the fictionalized one. Would you prefer the story you have created or the life you have lived? The answer to that question might surprise you. You might find that the life you have lived is so rich in spite of (or *because* of) your brokenness that you wouldn't trade it.

Sound Expression

Toning. To put it simply, "toning" is creating an extended sound using a single vowel. Toning does not require words or melody or singing; it's meditation in sound. Basically, if you can moan, you can tone. David Gordon, a professional singer and voice teacher, points out on his website (www.spiritsound.com/toning.html) that toning with vowels such as "ah" or "ee" or "mm" sets up vibrations that literally massage your mind and body from the inside out, and can awaken and deepen your sense of self. He suggests starting by letting your intuition choose a vowel for you. Then, beginning in the comfortable middle of your vocal range, start to make your sound. Then try a lower pitch, then a higher one. If a vowel or tone doesn't feel "right," choose another. The important thing is to explore the physical and emotional sensations of these sounds and their effect on you.

Another possibility is to choose the primary vowel sound of your name. As you close your eyes and repeat the vowel, let it find its own volume and sound. Don't try at first to hold to a particular pitch. Rather, as you repeat the vowel, let it find its own natural pitch.

However you approach toning, you will be listening to yourself on every level. You may experience physical benefits, such as reenergizing your body and reducing stress. You may find that toning helps you release your physical and emotional pain. But most of all, you may experience a new awareness of your inner self and creativity that can help you move along your path toward mending.

Your theme song. Melodies have a way of sticking in our minds, and they often become associated with significant events in our lives. What if you were to create a personal melody that would be a "theme song" for you? You might experiment just humming something. Or, if you have a musical background, play around on a keyboard or flute or guitar. (There are now computers and inexpensive keyboards that record what you play, so you could replay your theme song whenever you wish.) You might add words to create a song to sing. Or, if you can't write or read music, select one of your favorite songs (or let it choose you) to serve as your theme song. Hum it from time to time. Reflect on why it is your theme song. When you find yourself depressed about your brokenness, having a theme song can soothe your spirit or (if your theme song is sad) help you get in touch with your pain.

Experiential Expression

Personal monologue. In the world of theater, a monologue is a dramatic sketch performed by one actor. You can create an on-the-spot monologue by thinking out loud about some aspect of your brokenness. Just speak the words aloud as you think of them. Then reflect on what it was like to hear your voice speaking words that might normally run silently through your mind.

Autobiographical theater. Consider writing a short one-act play about a key event in the formation of your brokenness. Then, if you feel comfortable doing this, invite close friends to join you in reading it aloud or even performing it (acting skill is not necessary!). When you assign people reading roles or cast them in various roles, consider casting yourself as the person who was your antagonist (if there was one) in your real-life story.

If it feels too painful to involve other people, consider writing a one-person play. If you have access to video or audio equipment, you might want to record yourself reading or performing your play so you can review it at your leisure. Journal about the experience (perhaps in your visual journal, if you have chosen to keep one). How did you feel while you were writing the play? While you were reading or acting out your story?

Your own comedy. It is often said that there is a fine line between comedy and tragedy. Briefly write out your life story with particular attention to events related to your brokenness. Then take this story and see if you can turn it into something that is humorous. Write a funny short story or develop a brief stand-up comedy routine about your life. Remember, there are a number of famous comedians who have made large fortunes from their misery. Can you think of any aspect of your story that you or someone else might be able to see as humorous? If you can find some humor, spend some time enjoying it. Does it change the way you see or feel about your brokenness?

Theater of the imagination. This suggestion may either be the easiest or the most difficult because it requires no external materials or locations. In this exercise, you simply transport yourself, via imagination, to your favorite place on the planet.

When I am feeling depressed or overwhelmed, I close my eyes and transport myself to the place I like best: Ghost Ranch in New Mexico. (As I thought about this, I suddenly realized that Ghost Ranch is also the locus of the disastrous accident I described in the first chapter). When I picture Ghost Ranch, I see myself sitting in an Adirondack chair in front of the dining hall. From there I can see the mountains. I can even "see" myself getting up and walking around to various buildings, to the ranch's Zen garden and its labyrinth.

So, if you take this challenge, close your eyes and see if you can visually explore your favorite place from the easy chair in your home. Don't limit yourself to visual images. Can you hear sounds related to your favorite place? Are there aromas you associate with it? Try using all five senses, including touch and taste. What would you be doing? You might try using an audio recorder to document the experience as you describe it aloud. You might use the recording for a guided meditation at a future date.

When your sense of brokenness overwhelms you and you just need to get away from it, using this form of creative visualization affords an opportunity to take an emotional vacation without ever leaving home.

⌘

As you consider these suggestions for your personal yoga of creativity, I hope that you will also explore the incredible range of your own expressions. Can you think of other benefits that creative expression might offer you in your quest for mending? If you are already practicing a form of creative expression, in what ways is this helping your mending process? Remember that being creative is ultimately believing that there are new possibilities out there! The key is finding a form of creative expression that lets you explore these new possibilities.

MAKING CREATIVITY INTO A PERSONAL YOGA

Now that you have explored some tools for creative expression, I want to offer several suggestions for ways to use these tools (and others of your invention) to sustain you as you continue to cope with and transcend your sense of brokenness. Transcending your broken-ness doesn't mean eliminating it or ignoring it. It means being able to find meaning in it and move on with your life not in spite of your brokenness, but with the personal insights you have gained from it.

If you have completed one or more creative projects, take a few moments to think about and feel the experience. Did your act of creative expression have any impact on your feeling of broken-ness? Was your anguish eased in any way? Did the creative expe-rience help you in some way to transcend yourself and your pain? I hope it did.

One step is to use the yoga of creativity to capture and act on impulses as they occur to you. You may want to carry with you a small notebook or sketchbook in which to make notes about an idea, an image, or a process as it presents itself to you. This is a good way to record possibilities in the rawest form. Write one sentence or even just one word to capture a story idea or poem. Draw a stick figure or outline to represent a drawing or painting you wish to make. Map out in a swirly diagram a dance you want to pursue.

When you are unable to write or draw, or when verbal expression better lends itself to oral expression, you can use an inexpensive audio recorder to document notes. Or you can use a camera or a cell phone to photograph something that catches your eye and inspires you. The same is true of a video camera. It can record visual motion and activity that might inspire the pro-duction of a play, a dance—even a short film.

Using your notes, drawings, recordings, or photos to capture your ideas and images will allow you to return to them later, when you can spend time considering how these ideas relate to your brokenness, and whether creative expression can help you further your mending process.

Try to work with your creativity on a regular basis, weekly or daily if you can. Still, don't be surprised if creative impulses don't show up in your consciousness every day. I find that cre-ative ideas arrive periodically, with days and sometimes weeks between them. Even if ideas don't present themselves on a daily basis, you can collect small inspirations as they occur around you and store them to dip into later for expressive projects.

I also suggest that you look for ways to use your creativity to work with other tools we explored in this book. For example, you might use a visual journal in conjunction with a weekly Sabbath experience. Or combine a dance with a journey through a labyrinth. Or use a drama that you write in conjunction with a *Lectio Divina* exploration. You could turn the process of finding objects for your sculpture or your scrapbook into a pilgrimage. There are multiple possibilities. I hope you will explore many of them and add possibilities of your own creation that take you further along the mending way.

THE DISCIPLINE OF A SPIRITUAL PRACTICE

One of the important things to remember about artists, musicians, and other practitioners of the creative arts is that their expression involves not just expression, but also discipline and practice. The same is true of deeply spiritual persons. Their daily and weekly schedules provide room for the disciplined practice of spiritual tools. Discipline is key to any yoga practice as well, through a thoughtful, carefully planned routine several times a week, if not daily. It is this regular commitment to paying attention that will rekindle your creativity. If you decide to make creativity a part of your spiritual life, consider making it a true yoga, an ongoing, regular part of your life, just as you might for physical exercise or committed spiritual practice.

Here are some suggestions for developing your yoga of creativity into a disciplined spiritual practice:

A regular schedule. Just as in physical exercise, in order to reap the greatest benefit from your spiritual yoga, you need to set a regular schedule for creative expression and reflection. You might decide to practice at the same time every day or once a week. Several times a week might be a comfortable compromise if you are just starting out. Also, you may want to begin with a practice you already enjoy, such as writing in your journal. I have had success with what Julia Cameron, teacher, author, artist, poet, playwright, novelist, filmmaker, composer, and journalist, calls "morning pages" in her bestselling book, *The Artist's Way*. Morning pages are a set of three handwritten pages that you faithfully complete every morning, which requires a daily commitment to "show up" for the process. As Cameron puts it, "Creativity lies not in the done but in doing."

The same is true with the yoga of creativity. You need to regularly show up for the process. It may take a while to make your yoga of creativity part of your regular spiritual practice, but over time you may well come to anticipate it with joyful expectation. So I urge you to get out your calendar or planner and start assigning time to your yoga of creativity.

Commitment. In order to develop an ongoing program of spiritual practice, it is necessary to make a commitment to the process. Commitment first of all means making a decision to pursue a practice. Second, it requires determination and sometimes sacrifice. If you're the kind of person who wouldn't think of ignoring an important business meeting, a test, or a doctor's appointment, think of applying that same level of commitment to the times you set aside for your spiritual practice. If you're thinking, "I just don't have time for creativity or another form of spiritual practice," it may be necessary to recognize that you are going to have to give up something in order to add something to your schedule. You may need to forgo watching one of your favorite TV programs. You may need to give up a half hour of sleep in order to have time for your practice. I would suggest looking at your weekly schedule to determine what you can sacrifice with the least amount of discomfort.

In *Soul Fire: Accessing Your Creativity*, Thomas Ryan compares the creative energies we have as children with puppies romping in the yard: "But when we grow up, they bark like dogs in a kennel—leaping and yapping to be uncollared, to be let out to run in the beckoning sunlight and open fields or flat expanses of beach. But if this is to happen, something has to give—the equivalent of a leash, a collar, a locked gate. Something has to shift to make way—an agenda book, a routine of evenings spent staring passively at the tube, an image of ourselves and of what we are capable."

Consider this: whatever you need to shift to create a time for a disciplined spiritual practice may be well worth the reward of unlocked creativity.

Attention. Like any spiritual practice, your yoga of creativity is a living thing, and living things need attention and care. Be careful not only to pursue your creative expression but also to spend time thinking about and feeling it. Use your sketchbook or your journal to reflect on what you are experiencing. As you reflect, don't be afraid to modify your yoga of creativity if it isn't working. Stay with your practice for a period of time to make sure you aren't abandoning a process that may be helpful after some period of time, but don't be afraid to change your expressive tools in the same way that you might change medicines if the one you are taking isn't helping. Consider also changing the time of day (or the day itself) that you devote to your yoga, or change from one practice to another. As you reflect on your process, pay careful and caring attention to the nuances of how you are feeling and what impact your yoga of creativity is having on your experience of brokenness.

TURNING WOUNDS INTO LIGHT

I want to insert one additional suggestion before the close of this chapter. As with the other tools in this book, the yoga of creativity may sometimes bring up images or emotions that are profoundly disturbing or overwhelming. If that is the case, yet you feel that the creative process might be helpful to your mending, I encourage you to seek the services of a professional in the field of creative arts therapy. There are essentially as many forms of creative arts therapy as there are types of creative expression. In addition to art therapy, you can also access music therapy, dance/movement therapy, poetry therapy, and drama therapy.

All of the creative arts therapies specialize in understanding and utilizing expressive arts experiences to benefit physical, mental, emotional, and spiritual health. The creative arts therapies are founded on the belief that engaging in the creative process is healing and life-enhancing. With the guidance of a specifically trained creative arts therapist, the various art forms are made accessible regardless of your experience or level of talent. Reflecting on the process and the product can also lead to new insights, feelings, and skills that can transfer into a more wholesome and gratifying sense of self and how you relate to the world. As twentieth-century cubist artist Georges Braque once said, "Art is a wound turned into light."

If you decide to seek the services of a creative arts therapist, make sure that you find not just an artist but a professional with therapy skills training. If you think of asking an artist (or musician or dancer) for help, remember that an artist is not trained in the therapeutic applications of art. You would contact a professional in the arts for advice on techniques and aesthetics, but for arts-related therapy, you will want to contact a trained and credentialed creative arts therapist. (For more information about this, visit the website of the National Coalition of Creative Arts Therapies Association, www.nccata.org.)

Though your process of mending may continue throughout your life, transcending yourself through creativity can not only help you gain a sense of closure about the most immediate aspects of your brokenness, but also help you begin to move past your inward gaze and connect with the community around you. That connection to community is the next step in the mending process. This shift from inward to outward leads you to the final chapter in the mending experience.

8

THE "THIRD JEWEL"
Sharing Your Brokenness

THE IMPORTANCE OF COMMUNITY

Sometimes we spend so much time focusing on mending our brokenness that we fail to realize that there is a gift in it: we meet at the broken places. Our brokenness is like a crack in a wall that separates us from other people. It allows us to connect with others who are suffering. And we need to be among others of our kind. Connecting and belonging are as much a human need as are breathing and eating and sleeping. This is the importance of community.

The spiritual tools in the previous chapters have mostly been designed to be used on your own. However, it is important to recognize that we ultimately come to know who we are not by ourselves, but through relationships. Some of those relationships involve just two people. Others require interaction with more than two people, usually individuals who have some kind of common interest, connection, or responsibility—in other words, a community. Establishing such a community is about finding a place, a group where you belong. It is also about making connections and creating relationships with individual members of that group.

In a unique way, community may be one of our most important spiritual practices. Think about it: if you revere a sacred figure and observe a system of ethical and ritual practices, you have a personal belief system. Many people have such practices. But when individuals come together seeking common ground in belief and practice, something special happens. As they share ideas, worship together, and learn together, they start to look beyond themselves as separate individuals. A special bond occurs that connects them not only with each other but also with the Transcendent.

Ultimately we cannot truly mend ourselves without some connection to and support from a community. Fully participating in a community provides the support we need for our ongoing journey. Being part of a community can be a great comfort and an important teacher in our mending. Connecting to community also gives us the opportunity to share with others the coping skills we have learned. Best of all, feeling like part of a community can empower us to offer support to others who are in need.

Yet even as I say this, I would be less than truthful if I told you that my process with community is complete. In fact, I find it very difficult to be part of a social group, and it is even harder for me to entrust my well-being to another human being—yet alone rely on a community for care or be a helpful part of a community. Even as I struggle with this, I understand today more than ever the important role that being part of a community can play in dealing with brokenness.

No matter how many tools I found to help me cope with my brokenness, I still felt that something was missing. I now see that community, like the "pearl of great price" mentioned in the Christian scriptures, is something of great value for anyone seeking wholeness.

Community may not be literally a pearl, but according to Buddhist teaching, it is a jewel. In fact, it is one of what Buddhists call the "Three Jewels": the Buddha, the Dharma, and the *Sangha*. The Buddha, of course, is the one who achieved enlightenment and set about sharing with the rest of the world how they, too, could achieve enlightenment and end their suffering. I would describe the Dharma as the set of teachings, or better yet, the healthy way of living open to those who embrace Buddhism. The *Sangha* is the coming together of the individuals who accept Buddhism as a community, who work together to support each other, and the monk or nun who leads them.

In his wonderfully clear and simple book *The Heart of the Buddha's Teaching*, the Vietnamese Buddhist monk Thich Nhat Hanh describes the importance of each of these "Three Jewels" and what it means to take refuge in each. Taking refuge in the Buddha, he writes, enables us to "trust in our capacity to walk in the direction of beauty, truth and deep understanding." Taking refuge in the Dharma, we "enter the path of transformation, the path to end suffering." Taking refuge in the *Sangha*, we devote ourselves to building a community in which we can dwell in "mindfulness, harmony, and peace."

Here's what Hanh has to say about the practice of *Sangha* (I have substituted the word "community" for the word *"Sangha"*):

> It is well worth investing in a community…. [I]f you select a fertile field and invest your wonderful seeds in it, the harvest will be bountiful. Building a community, supporting a community, being with a community, receiving the support and guidance of a community is the practice…. We have individual eyes and community eyes. When a community shines its light on our personal views, we see more clearly. In the community, we won't fall into negative habit patterns. Stick to your community. Take refuge in your community and you'll have the wisdom and support you need.

Virtually all organized forms of spiritual practice include similar components: a figure to be revered (Buddha, God, the Higher Power); a set of teachings or guidelines for living (the Dharma, the Torah, the Gospels, the Qur'an); and some form of community. In fact, these three elements are essential to a religion, and they provide the basic tools needed for the spiritual journey.

In particular, all religions speak of the benefits of healthy community. Christians believe that wherever two or three believers are gathered, God is with them. The very identity of Jews is strongly attached to their vision of themselves as a community with shared history and values. Muslims know the value of supporting each other at critically important times, such as the month of Ramadan when all able-bodied believers fast from food and water from sunrise to sunset.

In *Joyfully Together: The Art of Building a Harmonious Community*, Thich Nhat Hanh devotes a chapter to "Healing Our Isolation," where he tells the story of Buddha's first disciples who formed the first *Sangha*. The Buddha describes them as "a community of people who know how to live the life of awakening." Hanh goes on to explain that *Sangha* is more than a community; it's a deep spiritual practice, "a place to practice for the transformation." In an interview for inmotionmagazine.com, Hanh gives us an important clue about the critical role of community in this transformation: "The collective insight is always deeper than individual insight. In the Buddhist community, the *Sangha* eyes are always clearer than the individual eyes."

There's a Buddhist folktale that illustrates the importance of the *Sangha* in supporting an individual who feels broken: One day as the Buddha was traveling, he stopped in at a monastery. All but one of the monks had gone out seeking alms. One monk was left behind because he was ill with dysentery. When the Buddha found him, the monk's robes and his bed were covered in filth. The Enlightened One asked the monk where everyone else had gone and why no one had stayed behind to take care of him. The poor, sick monk replied that, at first, the other monks had looked after him. However, when he failed to get any better, he told the others that he would care for himself. The Buddha cleaned him up, found him a new robe, and changed his bedclothes. When the other monks returned, the Buddha chastised them, saying, "If we don't care for each other, who will take care of us? If you revere me, remember that when you look after each other you are caring for me."

In *Friends on the Path: Living Spiritual Communities*, Hanh offers a helpful analogy about a rock and a boat that particularly relates to those of us who feel broken. He points out that if we throw a rock into a river, it will sink. But a boat can carry hundreds of pounds of rocks and not sink. "If we have a boat, we can carry our pain and sorrow, and we will not sink into the river of suffering." That boat is the *Sangha*, the community.

Recently I read about a group in Edinburgh, Scotland, who call themselves the "Scottish Wild Geese *Sangha*." They've chosen the symbol of wild geese because the geese embody the way that members of their *Sangha* try to care for each other. When wild geese travel, they fly in a "V" formation that creates an uplift for all the birds following the leader, making it easier for each of them. When the lead goose gets tired, it rotates to the back of the formation and another goose takes its place in front. If one goose gets sick or wounded, two geese will drop out of the formation and follow it down to help and protect it. They will stay with the goose until it is able to fly again, and then they will launch out with another formation or catch up with the original flock.

What a great image for a *Sangha*! For those of us dealing with brokenness, the journey can be a long one, and we may have to contend with many difficulties along the way. A *Sangha* not only brings us together with people traveling in the same direction and makes the journey a little easier, but it also can be a support in both good times and bad. And it gives us a place not only to accept help but also to offer help in return.

CONNECTING TO COMMUNITY

The spiritual practices and tools you have been exploring in this book may have brought you to the point where you feel prepared to seek the "Third Jewel," a *Sangha* where you can "take refuge." There are basically two ways of connecting to community: you can look for a community that already exists and become part of it, or you can create your own community by identifying people with whom you would like to share.

Finding an Existing Community

A good way of finding a healthy community is to open your eyes and ears and pay attention to what your friends and colleagues are saying about their own communities. When people find communities that are uplifting and healthy, more often than not they talk about them. Watch and listen for stories in your local newspaper, television, or radio that present portraits of groups that seem to embrace your values and beliefs. Pay particular attention to details that reveal whether a group or organization enriches the lives of its participants. You may want to look for groups that help individuals turn their focus from themselves to others, especially to those who are in need. Here are some of the community possibilities you might want to explore:

Religious groups. An obvious place to look for a community is a church, mosque, synagogue, or temple. If you already are part of an organized religion, there is usually a wide array of options open to you for finding community. These include scripture study groups, singles groups, service committees, educational efforts, cooperative daycare efforts, seniors groups, teams that visit the sick and homebound, dinner clubs, work projects, and mission trips.

Independent religious groups. An unusual and innovative option for community is a group of religious adherents who come together periodically, not in houses of worship, but rather in their own homes. These groups include nondenominational Christian bible study, the Jewish *chavurah*, or (in my own city) a group such as Independent Muslims of Louisville. Usually groups such as these meet once or twice a month for a potluck supper, study of scripture, discussion, ritual, and other forms of spiritual activity. One advantage is that such groups do not have the burden of having to adhere to a religious authority (as is sometimes the case in a church, synagogue, or mosque). Participants are free to express ideas that are controversial and to embrace practices that are outside the mainstream.

Nonreligious groups. Don't limit your quest for the third jewel just to religious organizations. Some of the most deeply spiritual experiences I have had came from groups that don't, on the face of it, have a specific religious purpose.

One of the most powerful spiritual groups I have ever encountered is Alcoholics Anonymous. There are AA meetings in virtually every town and village in the country, and usually more than one. AA is an organization that was created with a sole purpose in mind: providing those who suffer from the brokenness of alcoholism with the community they need to stop drinking and stay sober. If you are battling an addiction to alcohol, AA is a great place to seek help, but even if you aren't an alcoholic, you might want to find an "open" AA meeting so you can see for yourself how recovering alcoholics help each other.

If you aren't an alcoholic but have some kind of addictive problem, you might look for a group that uses AA's twelve-step process and its concept of community support to deal with other kinds of addictions, such as drugs, gambling, sex, or another problem. Also, Rami Shapiro's book *Recovery—The Sacred Art: The Twelve Steps as Spiritual Practice* (SkyLight Paths) presents the Twelve Steps of Alcoholics Anonymous as a spiritual practice that anyone can do to live a freer, more God-centered life.

If you are not struggling with an addiction but want to see if there is something in the twelve-step process that can help you cope with your brokenness, I suggest the book *The Twelve Steps for Everyone* by spiritual psychologist Jerry Hirschfield. You might also consider learning about Al-Anon, a group formed to help people who live with alcoholics or addicts.

Another suggestion is to find groups that involve people with interests, and perhaps problems, similar to yours. There are book groups that meet once a month or so. There are theater-going groups, groups that enjoy cooking meals, and others that like exploring restaurants. Choral groups offer a wonderful opportunity for community. They allow for creative expression and friendship at the same time. Creative writing and poetry groups are springing up around the country. Check your phone book, local newspapers, and the Internet for possibilities.

Volunteerism. One of the best ways I can think of to connect with a community is to look for volunteer opportunities. The help of volunteers is needed by just about every nonprofit group in the country, from schools and libraries to hospitals and arts organizations. The reasons people volunteer are almost always at heart spiritual. Joining a volunteer group instantly connects you with people who are looking beyond themselves and their own problems to help others. The volunteer spirit is actually contagious. See if you can catch it. And when you develop a good "case" of volunteerism, take some time to journal about the "symptoms": a better outlook on life; less concern for your own difficulties; and a sense of connection with those you serve, as well as the people and organization with whom you are volunteering.

Creating Your Own Community

Building a community from scratch is a very creative process, but it can also be very demanding and time consuming. However, if you have the energy and commitment to create your own community, you may find this the most enriching experience of all, simply because you can design a group and recruit participants in any way you wish. If you invent a group, it can address any interest or problem you want to explore with other people. You can set the timetable, the number and frequency of meetings, and the location. If this is a path you would like to explore, I offer some suggestions in the next section about ways to consider and build such a group.

CONSIDERING YOUR COMMUNITY EXPERIENCE

Before you make a decision about what kind of community you might benefit from, it is good to consider what you would like to experience in community. Note that I didn't say, "what you hope to get from community." Too often those of us who feel broken and are looking for help tend to see everything only in terms of how it can benefit us. We may see our participation in a community that way as well, but if we focus *only* on how a community can help us, we may be immune to the joy we could experience by sharing ourselves with the community, by contributing to it, and by helping others. On the other hand, be careful not to let your focus be *entirely* on other people. It is good to have a balance of interest in others and care for yourself.

As you begin your search, I recommend journaling about your process. If you are checking out existing groups, make some notes for yourself so you can evaluate which group might be best for you:

- How welcome do you feel in the group?
- What is your sense of how the group works?
- What do you understand the group's goals to be?
- How do you see yourself fitting in?
- How might such a group help you?
- How might you help others in the group?

If you think you might like to create your own group, take some time to journal about:

- What would being part of such a new community mean to you?
- What would you hope to learn from the experience?
- What might participation in this new group mean to those who join it?
- What characteristics might you want the participants to have? (It is good for members of the group to have at least one characteristic in common, such as a skill or an interest, so there is always something to talk about when the group convenes. Think about your favorite interest or activity and build your group around that.)
- How many participants would be ideal? (Establishing a threshold number can be helpful.)

- Write a brief, one-page description of the new group, its
  purpose, and how it would meet.

Once you have spent some time evaluating and journaling,
look around and begin considering which specific individuals you
might want to invite to be part of the group. Find like-minded
folks. Start talking to them. Share with them your one-page
description of the community you have envisioned. Seek their
advice about how to make participation in this new community
attractive to the people you want to invite.

Then take the next step and actually invite people to an initial meeting at which you can launch the group and set up its
ground rules and operating pattern. Make sure that the meetings
of your group offer some element of fun, or people will see this
as just one more task and stop coming. Set a next meeting date.
After you have met several times, periodically review how the
group is doing.

From time to time, take your own spiritual and emotional temperature and do the same for the group. What impact is your
involvement in the group having on your sense of brokenness?
What impact is your participation having on the others in the
group? Don't be afraid to change the way the group operates or
how, when, or where it meets. If it isn't working out, you may need
to let go of this pursuit and either try creating a different group or
join an existing one.

There's one more thought about communities I want to add
that has to do with our expectations for a group. As Buddhist
teacher Jack Kornfield so elegantly puts it in his book *After the
Ecstasy, the Laundry,* "If we go to spiritual community in search of
perfect peace, we will inevitably meet failure. But if we understand
community as a place to mature our practice of steadiness, patience,
and compassion, to become conscious together with others, then
we have the fertile soil of awakening. One Korean Zen master told
students that their communal practice was like putting potatoes in
a pot and spinning them around together long enough to rub off
all the peels."

I am reminded of the country-gospel song "May the Circle Be Unbroken." When we're looking for a community, many of us are hoping to find that circle, an ideal family where we will be welcomed and understood, where nothing can break it. But the reality is that the circle will experience brokenness, just as we individually experience brokenness. In his book *Blessed Relief: What Christians Can Learn from Buddhists about Suffering* (SkyLight Paths), Gordon Peerman, an Episcopal priest and psychotherapist, offers a healthy perspective to consider: "It is closer to the truth to say that the circle will likely be broken, that people will have their issues with one another. The question … is not whether there will be misunderstanding, conflict, or injury, but whether we will learn together how to repair the circle when it has been broken. It takes a commitment of spiritual practice."

SANGHA AS A SPIRITUAL PRACTICE

My own process of finding a community is by no means complete. Because of the work I do as an interfaith leader, becoming an exclusive participant in an existing group at a church, synagogue, mosque, or temple creates some problems for me. I do participate periodically in a *chavurah* and find the group challenging and rewarding, but because my participation is limited by the ever-increasing number of religious events I need to attend in our community, the *chavurah* isn't meeting my greater need for community, and I am not contributing to the needs of the group itself. More and more, I've been giving thought to creating my own community.

My spiritual director and I have talked from time to time about creating a men's group that could come together for walks, talks, and meals on a regular basis. But because he and I have been incredibly busy, we somehow haven't seemed to find the time to form that group yet. More recently, I have been tinkering with the idea of inviting friends to join me in a group built around my great love: watching movies. I need to spend more time journaling and talking about this idea, but I think that I can probably pull together a group of very interesting people to watch a film and then gather for coffee or a meal to discuss what the film means to them.

I can already see that I want to create a community that is diverse and culturally rich, with participants who vary considerably in age, religious practice (or lack thereof), educational background, and profession or avocation. I also want to spend some time thinking about how I can add an element to this group that connects the people in the group with the community, to address community needs or problems as well.

Notice that I haven't mentioned the word "brokenness" in anything I have said about the community I hope to create. I am talking about building a community around common interests, a joy in living, a desire to learn and explore, and most of all a concern about the people and world around me. Yet I also suspect that many of the people I invite may have some sense of their own brokenness. I don't know how we will meet each other's brokenness needs, but I do know that by "being there," by getting together on a regular basis, we will be richer for the experience and more ready to share our inner lives than if we never met.

Community doesn't happen in isolation. This leads me to add a word of advice. Many communities are forming online, in forums, on sites such as MySpace and Facebook, and in chat rooms. While these virtual communities can be a source of valuable information and places to connect with people of like interest, they are not a substitute for the kind of *Sangha* community I am talking about. Real community requires actual face-to-face interaction with live human beings. Telephone contacts, e-mails, and other forms of virtual contact can be helpful to a certain degree, but if community is to play a truly helpful role in your mending, it is essential that you find ways to publically share space with other humans, to be able to look into their eyes, to shake hands, to breathe the same air.

I have read that prisoners sentenced to solitary confinement find the lack of human interaction an almost unendurable form of punishment. Monks who choose to live as hermits follow regimens that provide opportunities for direct contact with other people from time to time. Even the most introverted of us are social animals. We need human contact in order to thrive. If we aren't nurtured by our family of birth, we often reach out to our extended family or create a family of our own by joining a community or developing our own.

The importance of community is illustrated by one of the key maxims spoken by members of Alcoholics Anonymous. They say that in order to stay dry there are only two things you must do: "Don't drink, and go to meetings." In other words, stopping drinking isn't enough; going to meetings matters. In a similar way, I think that all the practices in this book aren't enough to mend our brokenness; community matters.

Participation in a community isn't just one more tool you can use to help mend your feelings of brokenness; it is a tool that can help you use *all of the other tools* more effectively. Community is, in fact, the glue that holds all of the other spiritual practices together. Whether you choose to observe a Sabbath, embrace Buddhist meditation tools such as *maitri* and *tonglen*, engage in the ancient Christian practice of *Lectio Divina*, take a *hajj*-like pilgrimage, walk a labyrinth, or follow a yoga of creativity, you will find each much more fulfilling if you undertake it in the context of a community. A healthy community is where you can share what you have experienced and learned, where you can celebrate your successes, and where you can look for solace when you feel despair.

As I mentioned in the Introduction, the process of mending what is broken is a journey, not a destination. The seven steps for a spirituality of brokenness that I have outlined in this book are part of a lifelong process. You may have tried many or all of the steps, and I hope you have found some tools for mending. You may not be "healed," but I trust you have found some new ways of looking at yourself and loving yourself.

As you proceed with your journey, I would like to offer you a special benediction in words adapted from the poetry of the wonderful twelfth-century Sufi mystic Rumi. I hope they guide you safely on your way:

> *In humbleness, be like the earth!*
> *In tolerance for those who do you ill, be like*
>   *a gentle breeze!*
> *In generosity for everyone, be like the sea!*
> *In compassion for others,*
>   *And especially for yourself,*
>   *Be like the sun!*

Afterword

Through an odd set of circumstances, it turned out that I would be in New Mexico on the first anniversary of the accident that I mentioned at the beginning of this book, an accident that shattered my shoulder and saddled me with a complication that left my hand essentially unusable for months. The prognosis for the syndrome I had developed was grim. But as a result of a connection to a local hand surgeon, I got therapy that over the next nine months returned use of my hand to me. As the anniversary approached, I was able to see that my recovery had far exceeded expectations. Although I couldn't quite make a fist, I could do virtually everything I wanted or needed to do with my left hand. I actually felt joy that I could type, lift things, drive, and even make art using both of my hands.

A ritual was definitely called for. The first step for me was to prepare for this ritual with a visit to the Sanctuario, a church in Chimayo, New Mexico, where I had prayed for mending the year before. As a sign of my gratitude, I had left in the church a small silver amulet of a hand. Such tiny silver sculptures are called *milagros*, or miracles. These medals are left in the church by people who have experienced some measure of healing or mending.

143

I purchased a second *milagro* that I took with me to Ghost Ranch for the anniversary ritual. On the anniversary itself, I rose early and visited an incredibly beautiful canyon called Plaza Blanca above the town of Abiquiu. There I retrieved a small piece of weathered branch with a crack in it. That branch looked like the way my arm had felt after my accident. That afternoon I invited a friend to join me for the twenty-minute drive to Ghost Ranch, where I found one last element for my ritual in the gift shop. It was a wrapped handful of sage to be set afire and used as a smudge stick in a Native American ceremony of cleansing and healing.

I did not have a clear idea of what my ritual would be like, but I decided the first step would be to walk the labyrinth that sits at the base of towering Kitchen Mesa. I carried with me the weathered branch from Plaza Blanca and the smudge stick. I wasn't sure how I was going to use my time walking the labyrinth, but as I began moving, my mind returned to my fall, and I began reliving the events of the first few months after the accident.

I reexperienced the fall itself and the bumpy, excruciating ride to the hospital. As the course of the labyrinth twisted and turned, I recalled how I had languished for two days in the hospital before the surgery that finally replaced my shattered shoulder and fixed my badly broken wrist. As I slowly trudged along the labyrinth path, thunder from an approaching storm served as an appropriate soundtrack for the unfolding story.

I relived the adding of a cast to my arm, the pulling of staples from my shoulder, the comedy of trying to shower with a bag over my left arm. Then came the despair of having the cast removed in late August and waiting for the swelling in my left hand to disappear—but it didn't. As I neared the center of the labyrinth, with lightning flashing in the sky a mile or two away, I began to reexperience the depression and despair I suffered when I received my diagnosis of reflex sympathetic dystrophy, thinking that my life had radically changed for the worse— perhaps permanently. Then, suddenly, I reached the center of the labyrinth.

I stood in the circle at the heart of the labyrinth for a few moments. The time served as a kind of mini-Sabbath, during which I could catch my breath both emotionally and spiritually at this midway point in my symbolic journey through the labyrinth. After some peaceful time of quiet and reflection there in the center, I placed my bonelike branch on the sand before me and lit my smudge stick. For a few minutes, I let its smoke exorcise the darkness and pain from this wooden symbol of my brokenness. When I finished smudging, I just stood in silence for a while.

Then a gift arrived. That gift was the memory of finding a hand surgeon in late October who offered me hope that I would regain some use of my hand. I remember asking him directly if I would recover full use it. In fact, I asked the question a number of times. Each time, he replied, "It'll get better." The question that remained was, "How much better?" In the months that followed I learned the answer to my question.

As I headed back into the twists and turns of the labyrinth's path, I started reliving the mending process. From the first outbound step I made, I began feeling a sense of growing relief, just as I had when the physical therapy on my hand began to improve the use of my hand. In an interesting symbolic mirroring of my feelings, the smudge stick I carried stayed lit and continued to offer its comforting smoke the entire way out. By the time I reached the entrance to the labyrinth and stepped back into the world, I was smiling.

I invited my friend to join me for the final part of the ritual. Chased by storm clouds, we moved slowly the quarter mile or so to Ghost House, the actual location of my accident. As we walked, I had time to quietly consider the implications of the story I had just relived. I made a mental note to take some time later to write down the story of this ritual and to consider its implications using *Lectio Divina* and the immersion technique.

When we got to Ghost House, I stood in front of the door and placed my second *milagro* on the exact spot where I had fallen. As I stood in silence, my friend took my smoldering smudge stick and used its cleansing smoke to symbolically remove from me any lingering pain and darkness.

But there was one last thing I needed to do to complete this process. As I approached the final step in this ritual of closure, I took a moment to reflect on how far I had come in my physical mending. I also paused to consider what lay ahead for me in emotional as well as physical recovery.

With regard to my hand, it was clear that I was approaching the limits of mending. I still couldn't make a fist with my injured left hand, but I could complete just about any task I needed to complete, so I felt good. I had come to a point of acceptance about the fact that my left hand would probably never return to the state it had been in before my fall.

A few days after I returned home from New Mexico a friend asked how my recovery was going, and I told her that I had probably reached my limit but was happy with where I was. She said, "I hope you can still gain back the full use of your hand." I thought for a moment about what she said. And in the spirit of *maitri* (befriending my pain) and *tonglen* (taking on the pain of others and sending them only good), I replied, "You know, if I had my wish, I would stay right where I am and send the remaining part of my mending on to someone else who needs it."

It is possible that my physical mending may continue to some degree. I just don't know. But the acceptance that I now feel about the limits of my physical recovery is pointing the way for how I can cope with my mending from emotional brokenness. I have reached a point of at least partial closure about "The Basement Story" and its impact in my life. I will be using the tools we have worked with in this book. I will be searching for other tools from the world's great religions to help me with my continuing mending process. And although the emotional scars still show, I will be looking to find or make community. As I do, I hope that my focus will be as much on how I can help others as it is on how they can help me.

There was one final piece of the closure ritual at Ghost Ranch that I haven't told you about. After the smudging, after I left the *milagro* on the concrete at the exact spot where I had fallen, I stepped up and into the room in Ghost House where the disaster had begun a year before. I walked over to the light that I had turned off a year before and turned it back on. Then I walked out the door ... very carefully.

$\mathcal{A}dditional\ \mathcal{R}esources$

Introduction

Dass, Ram. *Still Here: Embracing Aging, Changing, and Dying*. New York: Riverhead Books, 2001.

> In this book, Ram Dass offers a philosophy for aging that teaches us how to diminish our suffering despite the aches, pains, and limitations of age. This becomes possible when we step away from the ego-self and into the soul-self, where we can witness our thoughts and emotions and evaluate their effects on us.

Lane, Belden C. *The Solace of Fierce Landscapes: Exploring Desert and Mountain Spirituality*. New York: Oxford University Press, 2007.

> This is the most beautifully written exploration of the reality and symbolism of wild places that I have ever encountered. Lane's reflection takes you deep into an understanding of the meaning of extremity and an exploration of Ghost Ranch in New Mexico.

Lemle, Mickey. *Ram Dass: Fierce Grace*. DVD. Directed by Mickey Lemle. New York: Lemle Pictures, 2001.

> *Ram Dass: Fierce Grace* is an engrossing, poignant meditation on spirituality, consciousness, healing, and the unexpected grace of aging that was named by *Newsweek* as one of the "Top Five Nonfiction Films of 2002." Best known for his 1971 bestseller *Be Here Now*, which was a spiritual touchstone of the era, Ram Dass became an inspiration to people across the globe.

Brokenness

Ford, Marcia. *Finding Hope: Cultivating God's Gift of a Hopeful Spirit.* Woodstock, VT: SkyLight Paths, 2006.

> Drawing from Christian and Hebrew scripture and the wisdom of spiritual teachers from all traditions, Marcia Ford helps you realize that we all can receive a gift of hope and grace from the Divine— we just need to be open to accept it.

———. *The Sacred Art of Forgiveness: Forgiving Ourselves and Others through God's Grace.* Woodstock, VT: SkyLight Paths, 2006.

> Through real-life examples, penetrating reflections, scriptural references, and practical suggestions, Marcia Ford offers a new perspective on forgiveness and reconciliation, an approach rooted in the Spirit that can be learned by anyone no matter how deep the hurt.

Kurtz, Ernest, and Katherine Ketcham. *The Spirituality of Imperfection: Storytelling and the Search for Meaning.* New York: Bantam Books, 1993.

> Through thoughtful commentary and more than one hundred fascinating stories (from many religious traditions), this book enables us to accept the inevitability of pain and failure so that we can ease our hurt and move toward serenity.

Marshall, Jay. *Thanking & Blessing—The Sacred Art: Spiritual Vitality through Gratefulness.* Woodstock, VT: SkyLight Paths, 2007.

> Through penetrating reflections and practical tips for uncovering the blessed wonder in our lives—even in trying circumstances— Jay Marshall shows you how to recapture the goodness, holiness, and abundance that saturate our world.

Spitz, Elie Kaplan. *Healing from Despair: Choosing Wholeness in a Broken World.* With Erica Shapiro Taylor. Woodstock, VT: Jewish Lights, 2008.

> Looks at brokenness as an inescapable element of the human condition and traces the path of suffering from despair to depression to desperation to the turning point—healing—when first-hand knowledge of suffering can be transformed into blessing.

Web Resource

www.helpforbrokenness.com

> Created and maintained by the author of this book, offers a one-stop shopping approach to information, practices, and resources related to all of the spiritual techniques explored in this book … and more. It also is the home for the author's blog on "A Spirituality for Brokenness."

Sabbath

Baab, Lynne M. *Sabbath Keeping: Finding Freedom in the Rhythms of Rest.* Downers Grove, IL: InterVarsity Press, 2005.
> This is a heartfelt, thoughtful, and most especially, helpful guide-book for all of us who need to slow down and take time to enjoy our relationship with the Transcendent.

Benson, Herbert, and Miriam Z. Klipper. *The Relaxation Response.* New York: HarperCollins, 2000.
> Similar to the practice of transcendental meditation, the relaxation response is a very simple form of silent meditation that offers spiritual, emotional, and physical benefits to those who follow its practice.

Heschel, Abraham Joshua, and Susannah Heschel. *The Sabbath.* New York: Farrar, Strauss and Giroux, 2005.
> I can think of no better introduction to the process of Sabbath-keeping than this short but extraordinary work by one of the twentieth century's most penetrating philosophers of Jewish spirituality. The book is introduced by the author's daughter, who is herself a wonderful philosopher and theologian.

Schaper, Donna. *Sabbath Sense: A Spiritual Antidote for the Overworked.* Minneapolis, MN: Augsburg Fortress, 2004.
> According to Schaper, Sabbath moments are any moments that actively include the presence of God. By presenting solutions to overwork, this book is the perfect answer to anxieties felt in two-career families.

Web Resources

www.practicingourfaith.org/prct_keeping_ways_ideas.html
> This page offers useful, specific information about how the Sabbath is observed in Judaism and Christianity, and how you can bring a simple, healthy Sabbath experience into your own life.

www.relaxationresponse.org
> If you visit this website, you will find all the information you need about how to begin a meditation practice that is easy to employ and very beneficial in relieving stress. It can also be useful in pain management. See *The Relaxation Response* listing above.

www.meditationcenter.com
> If you are looking for an online resource that explains what meditation is and how it is practiced in its many forms, this is the perfect site for you.

MAITRI AND TONGLEN

Chödrön, Pema. *Good Medicine: How to Turn Pain into Compassion with Tonglen Meditation*. DVD. Directed by Barbara Groth. Louisville, CO: Sounds True, 2006.

In this engaging, multipart video presentation of a retreat led by Pema, we witness America's first ordained Tibetan Buddhist nun relate the brokenness in her own life and how she came to use the practices of *maitri* and *tonglen* to transcend her brokenness in ways that we can employ in our own lives.

————. *When Things Fall Apart: Heart Advice for Difficult Times*. Boston: Shambhala, 2005.

According to Pema, there is only one approach to suffering that provides lasting benefit. In a truly counterintuitive way, that approach requires us to embrace our pain with an attitude of friendliness, and relax into the groundedness of our entire situation.

Thurman, Robert. *The Jewel Tree of Tibet: The Enlightenment Engine of Tibetan Buddhism*. New York: Free Press, 2006.

A veritable retreat in book form, it offers a practical philosophical and spiritual path to understanding the world and ourselves based upon ancient Tibetan Buddhist teachings.

Web Resources

www.spcare.org/practices/tonglen.html

This website offers you an additional approach to the practice of *tonglen* and is specific in its advice about how to undertake this Tibetan meditation technique for personal mending.

www.gampoabbey.org

This link takes you to the homepage of the abbey where Pema Chödrön resides. The site is filled with wonderful spiritual resources that communicate the deeply human and sometimes humorous flavor that Pema brings to the practice of Tibetan Buddhism in the West.

LECTIO DIVINA

Casey, Michael. *Sacred Reading: The Ancient Art of Lectio Divina*. Liguori, MS: Liguori/Triumph, 1996.

This work offers a bold and engaging examination of the Western practice of *Lectio Divina*, the medieval contemplative approach to sacred texts, including the Christian Bible and spiritual classics.

Diamond, James S. *Stringing the Pearls: How to Read the Weekly Torah Portion.* Philadelphia: Jewish Publication Society, 2008.

> Although written to help readers understand the weekly portion of scripture that Jews are invited to explore each week, this book offers insights, techniques, and tools that serve as fitting companions for the person employing *Lectio Divina* to explore scripture from any religion ... or their own life stories.

Guigo II. The *Ladder of Monks and Twelve Meditations.* Translated and with an Introduction by Edmund Colledge and James Walsh. Kalamazoo, MI: Cistercian Publications, 1981.

> These two short works together represent a major lighthouse for those beginning the practice of *Lectio Divina.* They demonstrate how prayer, knowledge, and expectant waiting can help us gain a much deeper understanding of any spiritual book we explore.

Vecchione, Patrice. *Writing and the Spiritual Life: Finding Your Voice by Looking Within.* Chicago: Contemporary Books, 2001.

> Each person's life is a web of stories waiting to be told. According to poet and teacher Vecchione, it's only when we tap into our inner spirituality that we are able to find our true voice, the voice that compels the soul to speak.

Web Resource

www.valyermo.com/ld-art.html

> This site offers a very complete explanation of how *Lectio Divina* is practiced in today's world. It also offers very specific advice on how to use *Lectio Divina* in a group setting, which can also be useful in creating a sense of community.

PILGRIMAGE

Coleman, Simon, and John Elsner. *Pilgrimage: Past and Present in the World Religions.* Cambridge, MA: Harvard University Press, 1997.

> This is the first book to look at pilgrimage through the multiple lenses of history, religion, sociology, anthropology, and art history as it maps the cultural imagination.

Cousineau, Phil. *The Art of Pilgrimage: The Seeker's Guide to Making Travel Sacred.* Berkeley, CA: Conari Press, 2000.

> Filled with stories and insights from major spiritual figures, this book is a wonderful companion to use as you plan, go on, and then reflect upon your own once-in-a-lifetime sacred journey.

Post, Paul, Jos Pieper, and Marinus van Uden. *The Modern Pilgrim: Multidisciplinary Explorations of Christian Pilgrimage.* Belgium: Peeters Publishers, 1998.
> If you are interested in learning more in-depth information about modern pilgrimages, these authors present a survey of contemporary pilgrimage practices.

Shariati, Ali. *Hajj: Reflection on Its Rituals.* Houston, TX: Free Islamic Literatures, 1994.
> Written for Muslims planning to undertake their once-in-a-lifetime journey, this work delineates all of the rituals associated with the *hajj,* and explains their spiritual significance in a way that can be transferred to your own pilgrimage.

Web Resource
www.philcousineau.net
> This site is a wonderful resource not only for information about pilgrimage, but also for spirituality, creativity, and a number of other topics. Its links to other spirituality web sites are invaluable.

LABYRINTH

Artress, Lauren. *Walking a Sacred Path: Rediscovering the Labyrinth as a Spiritual Practice.* New York: Riverhead Books, 2006.
> This is the best book about labyrinths I have ever encountered. It clearly and concisely explains the origins, history, and use of the labyrinth as a spiritual tool whose impact reaches across geographic and religious boundaries.

Schaper, Donna, and Carole Ann Camp. *Labyrinths from the Outside In: Walking to Spiritual Insight—A Beginner's Guide.* Woodstock, VT: SkyLight Paths, 2000.
> This work is especially good for people who need an introduction to labyrinths. Unlike many self-help books, this one doesn't offer to change your whole life, just to reorient and reframe it in useful concentric circles that both take you deeper inside and allow you to go to your outer life more enriched as well.

West, Melissa Gayle. *Exploring the Labyrinth: A Guide to Healing and Spiritual Growth.* New York: Broadway Books, 2002.
> With practical advice and helpful resources, Melissa Gayle West blends the timeless wisdom and meaning derived from labyrinths. You will be introduced to specific ways to use the labyrinth for rituals, meaningful celebrations, spiritual growth, healing work, creativity enhancement, and goal setting.

Web Resource

http://veriditas.org

> Operated by Lauren Artress, author of *Walking a Sacred Path: Rediscovering the Labyrinth as a Spiritual Practice*, this is another one-stop shopping site, filled with everything you need to make labyrinth walking a part of your spiritual practice.

CREATIVITY

Capacchione, Lucia. *The Creative Journal: The Art of Finding Yourself.* North Hollywood, CA: Newcastle Publishing, 1989.

> Written by a widely respected art therapist, this book offers an approach to using art therapy for self-discovery and can be an extremely useful tool in helping you connect body, mind, and spirit on a daily basis through a full spectrum of creative expressions.

Ryan, Thomas. *Soul Fire: Accessing Your Creativity.* Woodstock, VT: SkyLight Paths, 2008.

> This is an inspiring guide to cultivating your creative spirit as a way to encourage personal growth, enrich your spiritual life, and deepen your communion with God. I think you will find it an invigorating call to set free your creative potential.

SARK. *A Creative Companion: How to Free Your Creative Spirit.* Berkeley, CA: Celestial Arts, 1991.

> As creative and inviting in its physical appearance (the text is presented in the author's handwriting) as it is in the exercises it offers to help spark your creativity, this book can be a joyful and joy-producing friend to accompany you on your journey to mending.

Sharp, Sharon, ed. *Expressive Arts Therapy: Creative Process in Art and Life.* Boone, NC: Parkway Publishers, 2002.

> The value of this book, which was compiled by a group of artists and therapists, lies in its invitation to employ creative activities that span the full spectrum of creative expression: writing, art, music, dance ... and more.

Web Resources

www.spiritsound.com/toning.html

> Check out this website for professional singer and voice teacher David Gordon's helpful ways to use toning as a yoga practice.

www.minddisorders.com/Br-Del/Creative-therapies.html

> Here you will find clear explanations of creative therapies, how they are used, how they can benefit you, and what to be careful about in their practice.

www.nccata.org
> This is the website for the National Coalition of Creative Arts Therapies Associations. It contains information on music therapy, dance/movement therapy, drama therapy, psychodrama, and poetry therapy.

COMMUNITY

Grateful Members. *The Twelve Steps for Everyone ... Who Really Wants Them*. Center City, MN: Hazelden, 1990.
> The Grateful Members make available to all of us the benefits and insights from the twelve-step program originally developed for alcoholics moving into recovery. It shows us how we can use the same process to confront, embrace, and move past whatever the brokenness is that plagues our lives.

Meyer, Richard C. *Step Up: A Vital Process for Spiritual Renewal*. Minneapolis: Augsburg Fortress, 2005.
> This book also shows how the twelve steps can be a tool for spiritual mending for everyone. The author divides the process into four phases: the Give-Up Steps, the Clean-Up Steps, the Make-Up Steps, and the Keep-It-Up Steps, describing how the steps can be used individually, with a partner, or in a small group to bring about personal transformation.

Shapiro, Rami. *Recovery—The Sacred Art: The Twelve Steps as Spiritual Practice*. Woodstock, VT: SkyLight Paths, 2009.
> Explores and employs the Twelve Steps of Alcoholics Anonymous from a deeply spiritual perspective that draws upon the insights and practices of Christianity, Hinduism, Judaism, Buddhism, Taoism, and Islam.

Vanier, Jean. *From Brokenness to Community*. Mahwah, NJ: Paulist Press, 1992.
> Vanier does not romanticize community. For him, community is a place of struggle and sometimes of conflict. Community is a place where the ego dies, a place of surrender. However, it is also a place of celebration, joy, and, ultimately, human fulfillment.

Web Resources

http://larcheusa.org/communities.html
> The L'Arche groups are built around service to and community with persons who have developmental disabilities. Although they relate to one particular type of brokenness, their spirit of community illustrates how brokenness can lead to powerful, positive ways of living.

www.taize.fr

Taize is an ecumenical monastic community located in France that draws persons from all religions and from throughout the world. Its spirituality is deeply rooted in music, creativity, and meditation and offers a model that can be duplicated in your own locale.

WORLD RELIGIONS

Bhaskarananda, Swami. *Essentials of Hinduism: A Comprehensive Overview of the World's Oldest Religion.* Seattle, WA: Viveka Press, 2002.

This book was recommended to me by a Hindu friend as a rich but easily understandable introduction to the world's oldest and perhaps most complex major religion.

Esposito, John L. *Islam: The Straight Path.* New York: Oxford University Press, 2004.

Embraced by Islamic scholars, this book offers an introduction to the beliefs and practices of the practitioners of the world's second largest religion, with information that you can use to address your spiritual needs.

Hanh, Thich Nhat. *The Heart of the Buddha's Teaching.* New York: Broadway Books, 1999.

Thich Nhat Hanh is one of the most universally respected leaders in Buddhism today, and in this book he explains the challenging ideas and practices of Buddhism in a way that simplifies them, and he offers specific ideas for how to apply them in our day-to-day lives.

Kushner, Lawrence. *Jewish Spirituality: A Brief Introduction for Christians.* Woodstock, VT: Jewish Lights, 2002.

This book is a window into the Jewish soul that people of all religions can understand and enjoy. Kushner shows us how to use the fundamentals of Jewish spirituality to enrich our own lives.

Peerman, Gordon. *Blessed Relief: What Christians Can Learn from Buddhists about Suffering.* Woodstock, VT: SkyLight Paths, 2008.

This is an insightful, compassionate presentation of nine Buddhist practices that can bring "blessed relief" to a wide range of human suffering. Peerman, who teaches mindfulness-based stress reduction at the Vanderbilt Center for Integrative Health, artfully shares practical techniques and skills to reduce your experience of suffering.

Smith, Huston. *The World's Religions: Our Great Wisdom Traditions.* New York: HarperOne, 1991.

Smith's book on world religions is the one that is most widely read. It is written by someone who not only studies religions but also brings the practices of the world's religions into his own life. It contains great information about beliefs, but not as much about spiritual practices.

Web Resources

www.beliefnet.org
> Beliefnet is one of the most popular websites related to spirituality. It is a great resource on the full spectrum of questions related to spirituality, religion, and personal problems.

www.religioustolerance.org
> This site is a great source of general information about the world's religions and seems to be free of any bias. It also contains links to other sites that contain more specific information about individual religions and spiritual practices today.

STORIES FROM WORLD RELIGIONS

Buber, Martin. *Tales of the Hasidim.* New York: Schocken Books, 1991.
> Martin Buber was one of the great Jewish thinkers of the twentieth century, and in this large compendium of stories he communicates much of what informs Jewish belief and practice today.

Bushnaq, Iner, trans. and ed. *Arab Folktales.* New York: Pantheon Books, 1987.
> A short but engaging collection of stories related to Arabs and Islamic spirituality.

Martin, Rafe. *The Hungry Tigress: Buddhist Myths, Legends, and Jataka Tales.* Somerville, MA: Yellow Moon Press, 1999.
> A rich, though brief, compilation of folktales drawn from South Asia used to teach children and adults major precepts of Buddhist morality and how to address and overcome suffering.

Voragine, Jacobus de. *The Golden Legend: Readings on the Saints.* Translated by William Granger Ryan. 2 vols. Princeton, NJ: Princeton University Press, 1995.
> This is the authoritative compilation of Christian stories and legends upon which has been formed much of what Christians believe, and even more of what makes Western literature so richly rooted in Christian stories.

Spirituality

Next to Godliness: Finding the Sacred in Housekeeping
Edited and with Introductions by Alice Peck
Offers new perspectives on how we can reach out for the Divine.
6 x 9, 224 pp, Quality PB, 978-1-59473-214-0 **$19.99**

Bread, Body, Spirit: Finding the Sacred in Food
Edited and with Introductions by Alice Peck
Explores how food feeds our faith. 6 x 9, 224 pp, Quality PB, 978-1-59473-242-3 **$19.99**

Renewal in the Wilderness: A Spiritual Guide to Connecting with God in the Natural World *by John Lionberger*
Reveals the power of experiencing God's presence in many variations of the natural world. 6 x 9, 176 pp, b/w photos, Quality PB, 978-1-59473-219-5 **$16.99**

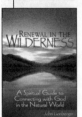

Honoring Motherhood: Prayers, Ceremonies and Blessings
Edited and with Introductions by Lynn L. Caruso
Journey through the seasons of motherhood. 5 x 7¼, 272 pp, HC, 978-1-59473-239-3 **$19.99**

Soul Fire: Accessing Your Creativity *by Rev. Thomas Ryan, CSP*
Learn to cultivate your creative spirit. 6 x 9, 160 pp, Quality PB, 978-1-59473-243-0 **$16.99**

Technology & Spirituality: How the Information Revolution Affects Our Spiritual Lives *by Stephen K. Spyker* 6 x 9, 176 pp, HC, 978-1-59473-218-8 **$19.99**

Money and the Way of Wisdom: Insights from the Book of Proverbs
by Timothy J. Sandoval, PhD 6 x 9, 192 pp, Quality PB, 978-1-59473-245-4 **$16.99**

Awakening the Spirit, Inspiring the Soul
30 Stories of Interspiritual Discovery in the Community of Faiths
Edited by Brother Wayne Teasdale and Martha Howard, MD; Foreword by Joan Borysenko, PhD
6 x 9, 224 pp, HC, 978-1-59473-039-9 **$21.99**

Creating a Spiritual Retirement: A Guide to the Unseen Possibilities in Our Lives
by Molly Srode 6 x 9, 208 pp, b/w photos, Quality PB, 978-1-59473-050-4 **$14.99**
HC, 978-1-893361-75-1 **$19.95**

Finding Hope: Cultivating God's Gift of a Hopeful Spirit
by Marcia Ford 8 x 8, 200 pp, Quality PB, 978-1-59473-211-9 **$16.99**

The Geography of Faith: Underground Conversations on Religious, Political and Social Change *by Daniel Berrigan and Robert Coles* 6 x 9, 224 pp, Quality PB, 978-1-893361-40-9 **$16.95**

Jewish Spirituality: A Brief Introduction for Christians *by Lawrence Kushner*
5½ x 8½, 112 pp, Quality PB, 978-1-58023-150-3 **$12.95** *(A book from Jewish Lights, SkyLight Paths' sister imprint)*

Journeys of Simplicity: Traveling Light with Thomas Merton, Bashō, Edward Abbey, Annie Dillard & Others *by Philip Harnden*
5 x 7¼, 144 pp, Quality PB, 978-1-59473-181-5 **$12.99** 128 pp, HC, 978-1-893361-76-8 **$16.95**

Keeping Spiritual Balance As We Grow Older: More than 65 Creative Ways to Use Purpose, Prayer, and the Power of Spirit to Build a Meaningful Retirement
by Molly and Bernie Srode 8 x 8, 224 pp, Quality PB, 978-1-59473-042-9 **$16.99**

Spirituality 101: The Indispensable Guide to Keeping—or Finding—Your Spiritual Life on Campus *by Harriet L. Schwartz, with contributions from college students at nearly thirty campuses across the United States* 6 x 9, 272 pp, Quality PB, 978-1-59473-000-9 **$16.99**

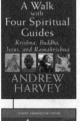

Spiritually Incorrect: Finding God in All the Wrong Places *by Dan Wakefield; Illus. by Marian DelVecchio* 5½ x 8½, 192 pp, b/w illus., Quality PB, 978-1-59473-137-2 **$15.99**

Spiritual Manifestos: Visions for Renewed Religious Life in America from Young Spiritual Leaders of Many Faiths *Edited by Niles Elliot Goldstein; Preface by Martin E. Marty*
6 x 9, 256 pp, HC, 978-1-893361-09-6 **$21.95**

A Walk with Four Spiritual Guides: Krishna, Buddha, Jesus, and Ramakrishna
by Andrew Harvey 5½ x 8½, 192 pp, 10 b/w photos & illus., Quality PB, 978-1-59473-138-9 **$15.99**

What Matters: Spiritual Nourishment for Head and Heart
by Frederick Franck 5 x 7¼, 128 pp, 50+ b/w illus., HC, 978-1-59473-013-9 **$16.99**

Who Is My God?, 2nd Edition: An Innovative Guide to Finding Your Spiritual Identity
Created by the Editors at SkyLight Paths 6 x 9, 160 pp, Quality PB, 978-1-59473-014-6 **$15.99**

Spirituality of the Seasons

Autumn: A Spiritual Biography of the Season
Edited by Gary Schmidt and Susan M. Felch; Illustrations by Mary Azarian
Rejoice in autumn as a time of preparation and reflection. Includes Wendell Berry, David James Duncan, Robert Frost, A. Bartlett Giamatti, E. B. White, P. D. James, Julian of Norwich, Garret Keizer, Tracy Kidder, Anne Lamott, May Sarton.
6 x 9, 320 pp, 5 b/w illus., Quality PB, 978-1-59473-118-1 **$18.99**

Spring: A Spiritual Biography of the Season
Edited by Gary Schmidt and Susan M. Felch; Illustrations by Mary Azarian
Explore the gentle unfurling of spring and reflect on how nature celebrates rebirth and renewal. Includes Jane Kenyon, Lucy Larcom, Harry Thurston, Nathaniel Hawthorne, Noel Perrin, Annie Dillard, Martha Ballard, Barbara Kingsolver, Dorothy Wordsworth, Donald Hall, David Brill, Lionel Basney, Isak Dinesen, Paul Laurence Dunbar. 6 x 9, 352 pp, 6 b/w illus., Quality PB, 978-1-59473-246-1 **$18.99**

Summer: A Spiritual Biography of the Season
Edited by Gary Schmidt and Susan M. Felch; Illustrations by Barry Moser
"A sumptuous banquet.... These selections lift up an exquisite wholeness found within an everyday sophistication."— ★ *Publishers Weekly* starred review
Includes Anne Lamott, Luci Shaw, Ray Bradbury, Richard Selzer, Thomas Lynch, Walt Whitman, Carl Sandburg, Sherman Alexie, Madeleine L'Engle, Jamaica Kincaid.
6 x 9, 304 pp, 5 b/w illus., Quality PB, 978-1-59473-183-9 **$18.99**
HC, 978-1-59473-083-2 **$21.99**

Winter: A Spiritual Biography of the Season
Edited by Gary Schmidt and Susan M. Felch; Illustrations by Barry Moser
"This outstanding anthology features top-flight nature and spirituality writers on the fierce, inexorable season of winter.... Remarkably lively and warm, despite the icy subject." — ★ *Publishers Weekly* starred review
Includes Will Campbell, Rachel Carson, Annie Dillard, Donald Hall, Ron Hansen, Jane Kenyon, Jamaica Kincaid, Barry Lopez, Kathleen Norris, John Updike, E. B. White.
6 x 9, 288 pp, 6 b/w illus., Deluxe PB w/flaps, 978-1-893361-92-8 **$18.95**
HC, 978-1-893361-53-9 **$21.95**

Spirituality / Animal Companions

Blessing the Animals: Prayers and Ceremonies to Celebrate God's Creatures, Wild and Tame   *Edited by Lynn L. Caruso*
5¼ x 7¼, 256 pp, Quality PB, 978-1-59473-253-9 **$15.99**; HC, 978-1-59473-145-7 **$19.99**

Remembering My Pet: A Kid's Own Spiritual Workbook for When a Pet Dies
by Nechama Liss-Levinson, PhD, and Rev. Molly Phinney Baskette, MDiv; Foreword by Lynn L. Caruso
8 x 10, 48 pp, 2-color text, HC, 978-1-59473-221-3 **$16.99**

What Animals Can Teach Us about Spirituality: Inspiring Lessons from Wild and Tame Creatures *by Diana L. Guerrero* 6 x 9, 176 pp, Quality PB, 978-1-893361-84-5 **$16.95**

Spirituality—A Week Inside

Come and Sit: A Week Inside Meditation Centers
by Marcia Z. Nelson; Foreword by Wayne Teasdale
6 x 9, 224 pp, b/w photos, Quality PB, 978-1-893361-35-5 **$16.95**

Lighting the Lamp of Wisdom: A Week Inside a Yoga Ashram
by John Ittner; Foreword by Dr. David Frawley
6 x 9, 192 pp, 10+ b/w photos, Quality PB, 978-1-893361-52-2 **$15.95**

Making a Heart for God: A Week Inside a Catholic Monastery
by Dianne Aprile; Foreword by Brother Patrick Hart, OCSO
6 x 9, 224 pp, b/w photos, Quality PB, 978-1-893361-49-2 **$16.95**

Waking Up: A Week Inside a Zen Monastery
by Jack Maguire; Foreword by John Daido Loori, Roshi
6 x 9, 224 pp, b/w photos, Quality PB, 978-1-893361-55-3 **$16.95**; HC, 978-1-893361-13-3 **$21.95**

Prayer / Meditation

Sacred Attention: A Spiritual Practice for Finding God in the Moment
by Margaret D. McGee
Framed on the Christian liturgical year, this inspiring guide explores ways to develop a practice of attention as a means of talking—and listening—to God.
6 x 9, 144 pp, HC, 978-1-59473-232-4 **$19.99**

Women Pray: Voices through the Ages, from Many Faiths, Cultures and Traditions
Edited and with Introductions by Monica Furlong
5 x 7¼, 256 pp, Quality PB, 978-1-59473-071-9 **$15.99**

Women of Color Pray: Voices of Strength, Faith, Healing, Hope and Courage *Edited and with Introductions by Christal M. Jackson*
Through these prayers, poetry, lyrics, meditations and affirmations, you will share in the strong and undeniable connection women of color share with God.
5 x 7¼, 208 pp, Quality PB, 978-1-59473-077-1 **$15.99**

Secrets of Prayer: A Multifaith Guide to Creating Personal Prayer in Your Life *by Nancy Corcoran, CSJ*
This compelling, multifaith guidebook offers you companionship and encouragement on the journey to a healthy prayer life. 6 x 9, 160 pp, Quality PB, 978-1-59473-215-7 **$16.99**

Prayers to an Evolutionary God
by William Cleary; Afterword by Diarmuid O'Murchu
Inspired by the spiritual and scientific teachings of Diarmuid O'Murchu and Teilhard de Chardin, reveals that religion and science can be combined to create an expanding view of the universe—an evolutionary faith.
6 x 9, 208 pp, HC, 978-1-59473-006-1 **$21.99**

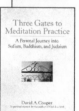

The Art of Public Prayer: Not for Clergy Only *by Lawrence A. Hoffman*
6 x 9, 288 pp, Quality PB, 978-1-893361-06-5 **$18.99**

A Heart of Stillness: A Complete Guide to Learning the Art of Meditation
by David A. Cooper 5½ x 8½, 272 pp, Quality PB, 978-1-893361-03-4 **$16.95**

Meditation without Gurus: A Guide to the Heart of Practice
by Clark Strand 5½ x 8½, 192 pp, Quality PB, 978-1-893361-93-5 **$16.95**

Praying with Our Hands: 21 Practices of Embodied Prayer from the World's Spiritual Traditions *by Jon M. Sweeney; Photographs by Jennifer J. Wilson; Foreword by Mother Tessa Bielecki; Afterword by Taitetsu Unno, PhD*
8 x 8, 96 pp, 22 duotone photos, Quality PB, 978-1-893361-16-4 **$16.95**

Silence, Simplicity & Solitude: A Complete Guide to Spiritual Retreat at Home
by David A. Cooper 5½ x 8½, 336 pp, Quality PB, 978-1-893361-04-1 **$16.95**

Three Gates to Meditation Practice: A Personal Journey into Sufism, Buddhism, and Judaism *by David A. Cooper* 5½ x 8½, 240 pp, Quality PB, 978-1-893361-22-5 **$16.95**

Prayer / M. Basil Pennington, OCSO

Finding Grace at the Center, 3rd Ed.: The Beginning of Centering Prayer *with Thomas Keating, OCSO, and Thomas E. Clarke, SJ; Foreword by Rev. Cynthia Bourgeault, PhD*
A practical guide to a simple and beautiful form of meditative prayer.
5 x 7¼,128 pp, Quality PB, 978-1-59473-182-2 **$12.99**

The Monks of Mount Athos: A Western Monk's Extraordinary Spiritual Journey on Eastern Holy Ground *Foreword by Archimandrite Dionysios*
Explores the landscape, the monastic communities, and the food of Athos.
6 x 9, 256 pp, 10+ b/w drawings, Quality PB, 978-1-893361-78-2 **$18.95**

Psalms: A Spiritual Commentary *Illustrations by Phillip Ratner*
Reflections on some of the most beloved passages from the Bible's most widely read book. 6 x 9, 176 pp, 24 full-page b/w illus., Quality PB, 978-1-59473-234-8 **$16.99**
HC, 978-1-59473-141-9 **$19.99**

The Song of Songs: A Spiritual Commentary *Illustrations by Phillip Ratner*
Explore the Bible's most challenging mystical text.
6 x 9, 160 pp, 14 b/w illus., Quality PB, 978-1-59473-235-3 **$16.99**; HC, 978-1-59473-004-7 **$19.99**

Spiritual Practice

Soul Fire: Accessing Your Creativity *by Rev. Thomas Ryan, CSP*
Shows you how to cultivate your creative spirit as a way to encourage personal growth.
6 x 9, 160 pp, Quality PB, 978-1-59473-243-0 **$16.99**

Running—The Sacred Art: Preparing to Practice
by Dr. Warren A. Kay; Foreword by Kristin Armstrong
Examines how your daily run can enrich your spiritual life.
5½ x 8½, 160 pp, Quality PB, 978-1-59473-227-0 **$16.99**

Hospitality—The Sacred Art: Discovering the Hidden Spiritual Power
of Invitation and Welcome *by Rev. Nanette Sawyer; Foreword by Rev. Dirk Ficca*
Explores how this ancient spiritual practice can transform your relationships.
5½ x 8½, 192 pp, Quality PB, 978-1-59473-228-7 **$16.99**

Thanking & Blessing—The Sacred Art: Spiritual Vitality through
Gratefulness *by Jay Marshall, PhD; Foreword by Philip Gulley*
Offers practical tips for uncovering the blessed wonder in our lives—even in trying circumstances. 5½ x 8½, 176 pp, Quality PB, 978-1-59473-231-7 **$16.99**

Everyday Herbs in Spiritual Life: A Guide to Many Practices
by Michael J. Caduto; Foreword by Rosemary Gladstar Explores the power of herbs.
7 x 9, 208 pp, 21 b/w illustrations, Quality PB, 978-1-59473-174-7 **$16.99**

Divining the Body: Reclaim the Holiness of Your Physical Self *by Jan Phillips*
8 x 8, 256 pp, Quality PB, 978-1-59473-080-1 **$16.99**

Finding Time for the Timeless: Spirituality in the Workweek
by John McQuiston II Simple stories show you how refocus your daily life.
5½ x 6¾, 208 pp, HC, 978-1-59473-035-1 **$17.99**

The Gospel of Thomas: A Guidebook for Spiritual Practice
by Ron Miller; Translations by Stevan Davies
6 x 9, 160 pp, Quality PB, 978-1-59473-047-4 **$14.99**

Earth, Water, Fire, and Air: Essential Ways of Connecting to Spirit
by Cait Johnson 6 x 9, 224 pp, HC, 978-1-893361-65-2 **$19.95**

Labyrinths from the Outside In: Walking to Spiritual Insight—A Beginner's Guide
by Donna Schaper and Carole Ann Camp
6 x 9, 208 pp, b/w illus. and photos, Quality PB, 978-1-893361-18-8 **$16.95**

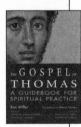

Practicing the Sacred Art of Listening: A Guide to Enrich Your Relationships
and Kindle Your Spiritual Life—The Listening Center Workshop
by Kay Lindahl 8 x 8, 176 pp, Quality PB, 978-1-893361-85-0 **$16.95**

Releasing the Creative Spirit: Unleash the Creativity in Your Life
by Dan Wakefield 7 x 10, 256 pp, Quality PB, 978-1-893361-36-2 **$16.95**

The Sacred Art of Bowing: Preparing to Practice
by Andi Young 5½ x 8½, 128 pp, b/w illus., Quality PB, 978-1-893361-82-9 **$14.95**

The Sacred Art of Chant: Preparing to Practice
by Ana Hernández 5½ x 8½, 192 pp, Quality PB, 978-1-59473-036-8 **$15.99**

The Sacred Art of Fasting: Preparing to Practice
by Thomas Ryan, CSP 5½ x 8½, 192 pp, Quality PB, 978-1-59473-078-8 **$15.99**

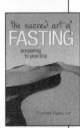

The Sacred Art of Forgiveness: Forgiving Ourselves and Others through God's Grace
by Marcia Ford 8 x 8, 176 pp, Quality PB, 978-1-59473-175-4 **$16.99**

The Sacred Art of Listening: Forty Reflections for Cultivating a Spiritual Practice
by Kay Lindahl; Illustrations by Amy Schnapper
8 x 8, 160 pp, b/w illus., Quality PB, 978-1-893361-44-7 **$16.99**

The Sacred Art of Lovingkindness: Preparing to Practice
by Rabbi Rami Shapiro; Foreword by Marcia Ford 5½ x 8½, 176 pp, Quality PB, 978-1-59473-151-8
$16.99

Sacred Speech: A Practical Guide for Keeping Spirit in Your Speech
by Rev. Donna Schaper 6 x 9, 176 pp, Quality PB, 978-1-59473-068-9 **$15.99**
HC, 978-1-893361-74-4 **$21.95**

About SKYLIGHT PATHS Publishing

SkyLight Paths Publishing is creating a place where people of different spiritual traditions come together for challenge and inspiration, a place where we can help each other understand the mystery that lies at the heart of our existence.

Through spirituality, our religious beliefs are increasingly becoming a part of our lives—rather than *apart* from our lives. While many of us may be more interested than ever in spiritual growth, we may be less firmly planted in traditional religion. Yet, we do want to deepen our relationship to the sacred, to learn from our own as well as from other faith traditions, and to practice in new ways.

SkyLight Paths sees both believers and seekers as a community that increasingly transcends traditional boundaries of religion and denomination—people wanting to learn from each other, *walking together, finding the way.*

For your information and convenience, at the back of this book we have provided a list of other SkyLight Paths books you might find interesting and useful. They cover the following subjects:

Buddhism / Zen	Global Spiritual	Monasticism
Catholicism	Perspectives	Mysticism
Children's Books	Gnosticism	Poetry
Christianity	Hinduism /	Prayer
Comparative	Vedanta	Religious Etiquette
Religion	Inspiration	Retirement
Current Events	Islam / Sufism	Spiritual Biography
Earth-Based	Judaism	Spiritual Direction
Spirituality	Kabbalah	Spirituality
Enneagram	Meditation	Women's Interest
	Midrash Fiction	Worship

Or phone, fax, mail or e-mail to: SKYLIGHT PATHS Publishing
Sunset Farm Offices, Route 4 • P.O. Box 237 • Woodstock, Vermont 05091
Tel: (802) 457-4000 • Fax: (802) 457-4004 • www.skylightpaths.com
Credit card orders: (800) 962-4544 (8:30AM–5:30PM ET Monday–Friday)
Generous discounts on quantity orders. SATISFACTION GUARANTEED. Prices subject to change.